BEING AND BELIEVING

Bryan Green

Former Rector of Birmingham

to

My Secretary
MARGERY NORTHCOTT

FORWARD MOVEMENT PUBLICATIONS

AUTHOR'S PREFACE

IN the modern world Christians must thoroughly know their faith, otherwise they will be unable to withstand other ideologies. They must also give a true witness in their lives, otherwise their religion will seem irrelevant.

Mark Guy Pearce once said: "The devil is the most orthodox person in the world." We believe that God is one, so the Epistle of St. James tells us, the devil also believes and trembles—but remains a devil. His belief doesn't alter his being. The two are meant to go together, being and believing. What we are is a sure indication of what we really believe; if we believe rightly and truly, then our lives cannot remain unaltered.

This little book of mine tries quite simply to set out some of the facts which Christians ought to believe, and some of the ways in which they ought to behave. Every reader will discover at once that the chapters are not a thorough study of the subjects with which they deal. They consist of a number of articles which have appeared week by week over a period of time in a popular British national magazine, *Women's Illustrated*. These articles have been revised with book publication in mind, and are now reprinted by kind permission of the Editor.

I hope that they will furnish some suggestions for thought and meditation, and it is for this reason that I have retained the suggested readings from the Bible which originally appeared beneath the articles.

For the thoughts expressed in this little book I can claim no originality, they are the product of books I have read and speakers to whom I have listened. I acknowledge particularly my debt to Bishop Gore's "Sermon on the Mount" and Dr. James Welch's "The Ten Commandments."

I must give my grateful thanks to my secretary, Miss

Northcott, for her work both on the original articles and on the preparation of the manuscript for the press, and to my publishers for their help in editing the manuscript for book publication.

St. Martin's Rectory,   BRYAN GREEN
   Birmingham.

CONTENTS

	PAGE
Author's Preface	3
Introduction	9

I THE BASIC TRUTH

Our United Declaration	12
God is Friendly	13
God is My Father	14
God's Power is Everywhere	15
God's Own Laws	17
He is the Maker	18
We can be Sure	20
Why Jesus is Different	21
What He Wants we must Want	22
This was Mary's Secret	24
The Heart of the Cross	25
Why Christ Came Back	26
Proof Positive	27
He Gives us Courage	29
Christ is Everywhere	30
God Understands	31
God Hates All Evil	33
He Longs to Help us	34
One Fold, One Shepherd	35
We are all His People	37
Friends with God	38
In Christ we shall Live for Ever	39
Life Everlasting	41

II THE WAY OF THE KINGDOM

A World-famous Sermon	44
The Blessed Life	45
Free for All	46
Pure in Heart	47
Salt of the Earth	48
Light of the World	49
The Kingdom of Love	50
Be Friends First	52
Live as a Child of God	53
Raise the Standard	54
Tit for Tat	55
Be Friends with your Foes	57
Money is a Trust	58
Do you Talk with God?	59
How to be Good	61
Singleness of Purpose	62
Serving One Master	63
God Knows our Needs	64
Search Your Own Motives	65
Withholding the Gift	67
Key to Availing Prayer	68
A Positive Rule	69
The Narrow Gate	70
The Test of Sincerity	71
Deeds—not Words	73

CONTENTS

III THE TOPICALITY OF THE TEN COMMANDMENTS

	PAGE
A Moral Landmark	76
The Word of the Lord	77
Be Right with God	79
Taking God's Name in Vain	80
Talking to God	82
Do you Give Sunday to God?	83
God Comes First	84
You and Your Children	85
Honour thy Parents	87
Crime or Punishment?	88
The Making of the Cross	89
Think Right	91
Honesty is the Best Policy	92
Don't Throw Mud	93
Seek God First	95

INTRODUCTION TO THE FIRST EDITION

FEW people would now say that what a man believes is of less importance than how he acts. Experience of totalitarian faiths has compelled us to recognise anew that how a man behaves depends in the not-very-long run upon what he believes.

This book is an expression of the compelling belief that Christianity is true: that we shall find salvation only through Christ, and that there is no lasting satisfaction for human beings except in obedience to His commands.

But how seriously we take His commands, and what success we have in fulfilling them in the rough-and-tumble of life, will depend upon how seriously we take His claim to speak with a more than human authority. If it be true, as Christians of many centuries, many races, and most diverse social circumstances have declared, that He came from God and opened the way to a new and enabling fellowship of man with God, thus bringing new spiritual resources to our aid, then His ethical teaching is challenging and may not be unrealistic. Starting with any lesser belief, His commands may be cherished as beautiful ideals, but are likely all too soon to be discarded as impossible dreams.

This consideration has determined the arrangement of the studies collected in this book. Beginning with the Creed and the way to God through Christ, they proceed to Christ's teaching about prayer and fellowship with God, and then turn to His teaching about how as His followers we ought to live. It is certain that we can so live only by the power and love of God.

The book ends with a study of the Ten Commandments in the social setting of our age. This may appear an anti-climax.

It is, in fact, the natural conclusion of the whole matter. Social life for free beings calls for ethical restraint. But experience shows that men discipline themselves not in submission to restrictive commands but in response to vital faith and in the process of creative living.

I
THE BASIC TRUTH

OUR UNITED DECLARATION

No one knows who wrote the Apostles' Creed.

There are only two certainties about it. The first is that the Apostles did not compose it; and the second is that the Apostles undoubtedly believed all that the Creed teaches.

It is probable, too, that this particular Creed was repeated, in early Christian days, by new converts at their baptism, and there is little doubt that in its final form as we have it, it reaches back at least to the fourth century.

This Creed is important to all of us for a number of reasons. It is very convenient if somebody asks, "What does the Christian faith teach?" to be able to reply, "It teaches this . . . ," and then to say the Creed.

There may be more to the Christian religion than is just contained in the Creed, but here its basic truth is expressed.

This Creed is important for another reason. We are all distressed these days—in a world where there is so much agnosticism and selfishness, and indifference to things that are spiritual—when we see the different Christian Churches and groups disagreeing with each other, and finding it hard to work together.

It is therefore a great encouragement when we come across two things upon which all Christians can agree—the Lord's Prayer, and the Apostles' Creed.

I do not mean by this that the Creed is said in all church services every Sunday; in some parts of the Catholic Church, like the Church of England, or the Roman Catholic, it is said every Sunday; but in others—for instance, the Congregational—it may be said but rarely, and is not an imposed test of orthodoxy upon the ministers.

Yet, in a general way, we all do agree with its teaching.

The Apostles' Creed is therefore our united declaration of our faith as Christians to the whole world.

We can rejoice and thank God that each of us is not the only Christian in the world—there are multitudes who believe as we do, and are trying, like us, to live by what they believe.

Suggested Bible reading: Ephesians, chapter 4, verses 1 to 7.

GOD IS FRIENDLY

"I BELIEVE in God." Of course you do. Most people can repeat with truth this first clause of the Apostles' Creed.

Mind you, their ideas of God may differ; but they do believe in God.

On the Gold Coast, for instance, the Ashantis believe that behind the whole Universe there is a far-away and distant Great Spirit. He is behind everything; only he is so far away that he doesn't bother—so the Ashantis don't feel they need bother about him either!

At birth the great Spirit gives to every baby a little of his own spirit—and there the matter ends. Between this one great Spirit and the world there are plenty of other intermediate spirits—in the trees, in the rivers, and most potent of all, the spirits of dead relatives.

Even the primitive sun-worshippers provide some evidence that they did not really worship the sun, but rather the Spirit behind the sun, the Creator of all.

Then there is the austere, mighty and all-powerful Allah of the Muslims. His will must be obeyed, and his will rules everything finally and inevitably—and Allah is good.

The Jews believe in a living God. He is good, and He is

powerful, and always at work in His world. He has chosen His own people, and He intends to use them for His purposes.

The Christian, too, believes in one great Spirit. The other religions have genuine glimpses, we believe, of the nature of God; but through Jesus Christ we believe that we can see and know Him more clearly.

To us God is not simply the Creator of the Universe. He is a kind and friendly Being. If we seek Him with all our hearts He will make Himself known to us, and "He will be our God and we shall be His people."

Suggested Bible reading: Isaiah, chapter 45, verses 5 to 18.

GOD IS MY FATHER

FOR most of us the word "father" is alive and full of meaning.

We think of him as the head of our home, the one who by his effort wins the money to buy food and clothing for us all. We think of his love for our mother, and their happy relationship together.

Here is strength and authority, someone who makes our family and home secure, someone to whom we can turn, and often do, in our major troubles and difficulties. As we grow older he becomes a very real companion and a fine friend.

This, and more, is what the word "father" means to so many of us. There are those, alas, whose experience is very different; those for whom the word conjures up a picture of someone hard and cruel who makes mother unhappy, and makes them frightened.

This indeed is true; but none the less it is exceptional. "Father" does stand for authority, strength and the kindly provision of life's necessities.

So we say, "I believe in God the Father." This should evoke in our minds the grateful thought of God providing for the needs of the children whom He has created, all powerful in His love and goodness, so that nothing in this changing world can alter Him.

His moral authority always stands over us in our sinning, in our failures. Because it is God's world, and He is good, sin and evil will never pay; they spoil us and in the long run they will destroy themselves.

We take this idea of God for granted far too easily. In no casual way should we say, "I believe God is my Father," but with awe and wonder and gratitude we should look to heaven and then, as it were, whisper, "God is my Father."

Here is the true confidence for life. Anxious and perplexed we often are, but He is still there; our Father is in control.

The small boy was frightened by the sudden storm. The ship was rolling and tossing. His mother saw his fear, and tried to comfort him.

"Mummy," he said, "is Daddy on the bridge?"

She knew that, as the captain, during such a storm he would be. She replied, "Yes, dear, he is."

"That's all right then," replied the boy, "I needn't be frightened any more."

Our Father is in Heaven, so why need we be anxious?

Suggested Bible reading: Philippians, chapter 4, verses 5 to 8.

GOD'S POWER IS EVERYWHERE

"GOD the Father Almighty." These words in the Apostles' Creed are often misunderstood—not so much the word "God" or "Father," but "Almighty."

Remember what we are saying. As Christians we affirm that we believe there is a God, a personal Being, a great Spirit, behind and above everything. We are sure, too, that He loves us; He is, in fact, our Heavenly Father. Then, we add, He is "Almighty."

Most people think that this means God can do anything at any time. When He doesn't do what we think He ought to do, we grumble and complain.

We ask petulantly in our human littleness, "Well, if God loves me as my Father why doesn't He do what I want? It's obvious that I need it."

Or more seriously, when we wrestle with the vast problem of human evil and suffering, our hearts cry out with deep perplexity, "If God is good, then why doesn't He do something about this evil? He can, because He can do everything."

Now, can God do anything at any time? You will answer, "Yes; what else can 'Almighty' mean?"

As a matter of fact, the word "Almighty" doesn't really mean "can do anything He likes," but, "all-powerful." In this latter sense it is quite true; it is God's will and power that created the Universe and holds it all in life.

He chose to have a world like ours, with the laws of Nature which were part of His plan. He chose to have in this world human beings like ourselves. How He created the world is another matter; but if we believe in God at all, we must believe that He chose to create it.

He is all-powerful, too, in another sense. If He so willed, the world would cease to exist. St. Paul told the Athenians quite bluntly, "In Him we live and move and have our being."

I don't want to bother you with technical terms, but if you are interested, we call these two ideas—the first picturing

God standing, as it were, outside and willing to create the Universe—His Transcendence; and the second, realising God's will ever actively choosing to sustain and shape this world, His Immanence.

Don't worry about these long theological words. Hold fast to the idea that God's power is behind everything. He loves us, too, so that we can trust our Father, who is both all-loving and all-powerful.

Suggested Bible reading: Acts, chapter 17, verses 22 to 23.

GOD'S OWN LAWS

LET us think again about the word "Almighty." I have explained how we think of God as being all-loving and all-powerful. Now I want to startle you.

God *can't* do anything He likes.

For instance, God can't make a circle a straight line, or suddenly cause all the stones to shoot upward against the law of gravity.

I am not being irreverent or blasphemous in saying this; I am just stating the sober truth. And it is superstitious and wrong to think otherwise.

It's like this. In the very act of creation, God has chosen to limit His power. By planning the laws of Nature in the way He has, He has, as it were, prevented Himself from doing certain things as long as these laws exist. He must not contradict Himself nor be inconsistent.

A more cogent example is God's gift to human beings of free will. So long as we are free to choose, He can't force our free wills; He can't make us love Him, and He can't make us good; He must leave the choice with us.

Don't misunderstand this, for God is still all-powerful, even if He can't do everything He wishes. The limitation of His power is something He has deliberately willed by creating the world and us. He has ordained the laws of the universe, and He keeps within His own laws.

Does this limit our prayers? Not very much, because we must always remember that there are still some laws of Nature, about which we know nothing. God knows all, however, and often what seems to us a miracle which contradicts the laws of Nature, is God working through laws unknown to us.

This means that, if we understand God's power aright, we shall not complain when God does not suddenly abolish all evil, or put an end to all war. And in our prayers we shall often ask God to show us if there is something we can do by our own free will to assist God's plan.

It is a wonderful thought that we are not God's machines or slaves, but His children, co-partners with Him in a co-operative effort to bring Heaven upon earth.

Only remember, we are junior partners, very junior. The secret of happiness is to let God always be the Managing Director of our lives.

Suggested Bible reading: Romans, chapter 11, verses 29 to 36.

HE IS THE MAKER

"MAKER of heaven and earth." By general consent the Bible story of the creation in the first chapters of Genesis is the finest of its kind.

Other stories about the beginnings of the world, the Babylonian for example, are crude by comparison.

In the Bible story one clear light shines throughout—a personal God is behind everything, and by His will all things were created.

It is not altogether easy to know how we are meant to understand these early chapters of Genesis. Christians have long differed about them—sometimes with unnecessary bitterness.

One view holds that we must take these stories literally, and that God's method of creation was exactly as the book of Genesis describes it. In that case there are obvious conflicts with much modern scientific teaching.

Other Christians believe that the Bible account of creation is a kind of allegory, something like the parable of the Prodigal Son. The inner truth is what God means us to grasp, while the outward form is a story or a parable; the details need not be taken literally.

This view does not conflict with the discoveries of Science. It enables the Christian to hold to the essential truth of Genesis, while accepting what science can tell us about the method of creation.

But Christians need not really argue about this matter at all, because the fact which really matters is basic to either view. However He did it, God created the world; He is the Maker of heaven and earth.

And what a great fact this is, if we believe it. We need not think that we are at the mercy of some blind, impersonal power. Behind all life is the will of a personal God, and we are His children, created in His image, objects of his love and care.

This, then, is the great fact that meets us in the first verses of the Bible and in the first clause of the Creed. God made us. Life is His creation, and we are His children.

Suggested Bible reading: Genesis, chapters 1 and 2.

WE CAN BE SURE

Believing that God is the Maker of heaven and earth, we may none the less sometimes doubt His love and goodness.

This is not surprising, for the world as we know it is often very hard, and some of us meet with more than our fair share of pain and suffering. Moreover, it often looks as if, when we pray to our Heavenly Father, nothing happens. How then can we help but wonder whether He loves us?

This has always been a difficulty for the religious believer and all the religions of the world bear witness to it. Men and women have wanted to believe that God is good and loving, but have often been perplexed. Religious teachers, prophets and leaders have tried to point the way to God, but there has been no certainty.

Christians believe that this is one reason why Jesus Christ came into the world. Man needed a response, definite and decisive, to his anxious search after the truth of God's goodness and love.

In the person of Jesus Christ, if we believe that He is God, we can see, and in some measure can understand, genuine goodness and perfect love.

It is this extra something, as it were, in Christianity which gives it its superiority and power over all other religions. It is for this reason, too, that the true Christian always wants to pass on his Christianity to other people.

He doesn't do it—or rather, shouldn't do it—in order to save them from hell, or because they are morally worse than he; he should do it simply because everyone has a right to know, through Christ, that God is good and that God is love.

I am sure as you read this you will notice that I have made one great assumption. I have said *if* God is like Jesus in character and nature we can be sure; that is why the next words in the Creed are perhaps the central rock of the Christian faith.

Suggested Bible reading: John, chapter 14, verses 1 to 7.

WHY JESUS IS DIFFERENT

"His only Son." What do we mean when we say that Jesus Christ is the Son of God?

To the trained theologian this can be a complicated and difficult question, but the simple Christian believer can understand something quite clear and definite about the statement that Jesus is the Son of God.

One of the essential qualities of being a person is that I have the power to reveal my nature and character.

Similarly we believe that God is self-revealing, and that He has revealed Himself in the person and human life of Jesus Christ. Here is a real man, but here also is God really showing His character and nature to us. Agreed that Jesus is a mysterious person; He is different from any one of us, because He is both God and man.

I am not going to explain the reasons why Christians believe this great and, in a way, almost unbelievable fact. They cannot be given briefly; but I do want to assert emphatically that all Christians should seek to understand the reasons, and to find out about them either by reading or by talking the matter over with a competent person.

But there is something more I must add, for the words "Son of God" mean more than just the fact that Jesus Christ was God and man. We are now facing the mysterious fact of the Trinity.

Within the Being of God there are, if I may put it like this, three centres of life, or "Persons" to use the theological term, though Person used of the Trinity does not mean an exclusive individual as it does when used of us. Each of the three Persons is God, and all are God. Before ever the world was created these three Persons were in a relationship of love one with the other, "Father, Son and Holy Ghost."

When therefore we state that we believe Jesus Christ is the Son of God we mean that He is God and that He is the second Person within the Being of God who came into this world, took our human flesh upon Him, and became man.

Don't be surprised if you find this difficult to understand. Christians, even the greatest theologians, have always found it difficult; and after all, it must be difficult, for what the nature of God is really like must always be beyond our human understanding. If we could understand God fully then our minds would be as great as His.

Suggested Bible reading: Hebrews, chapter 1, verses 1 to 14.

WHAT HE WANTS WE MUST WANT

SOMETIMES I think Christians talk too familiarly about Jesus Christ.

True, He was a man like ourselves, and in this sense we can think of Him as our elder Brother and as our Friend, very human and understanding; but He is also God, and as such claims our reverence and worship.

This point is made clear by the phrase in the Apostles' Creed, "I believe in Jesus Christ His only Son our Lord." He is the Lord Jesus, and as such has a right to expect the service of our lives and the homage of our lips.

It is all very reasonable. If Jesus Christ is God, then He can make a total claim upon our hearts' love and upon our lives. This He always did, and still does.

You remember how, when talking to the disciples on one occasion, Jesus said, "If a man love father or mother, wife or children more than me, he is not worthy of me." Human relationships are important, He says, but more important still is our relationship with Him. He claims first place, and claims it without hesitation.

This is a fact which Christians as a whole have largely forgotten. Fears and weaknesses we shall always have in our Christian lives, because we are human, but there is no excuse for the attitude that so many of us take, that our Christianity can be a kind of "extra" which we practise when we feel inclined.

If we are sincere at all in calling ourselves Christians, then we do accept Christ as our Lord and Master. This means, if it means anything at all, that we are prepared to put the will and teachings of Christ in the centre of our lives.

What He wants should be what we want; His Spirit should be the spirit that we show. The purposes and plans that He has for the human race should be the purposes and plans we should seek to make effective.

It is this total claim and demand of Jesus Christ which so many of us have forgotten; or if we have remembered that we have failed to acknowledge. It is only when Christians return to a simple acceptance of the lordship of Jesus in their daily lives that they will show the kind of witness which will attract the outside world to Christianity.

Suggested Bible reading: Matthew, chapter 7, verses 13 to 23.

THIS WAS MARY'S SECRET

"The birth of Jesus Christ was on this wise . . ." and then follows an extraordinary story.

A simple, but deeply devout, village maiden discovered she was going to have a baby. She was terribly perplexed, and very sensibly told her fiancé Joseph all about it. He was completely mystified. He believed in her innocence, but he knew the baby was not his. What was he to do?

Then Matthew tells us that God spoke to Joseph; and through this dream Joseph believed that this event was something quite out of the ordinary: it was God's own special doing. So Joseph married Mary.

At last the child was born, and His name was called Jesus.

This is what the Christian Church believes happened at the birth of Christ. When God took hold of our human flesh to become Man amongst us, Jesus was born of a human mother by the power of the Holy Spirit. His was a virgin birth.

Many people find this difficult to believe, because it is extraordinary, and, they argue, contrary to nature. But we must remember that Jesus Christ Himself is out of the ordinary and contrary to the natural order of things.

I have no doubt that God could have come into this world in some other way, but it seems to me that the evidence of the New Testament indicates that He chose thus to come among us, born of a virgin.

When one comes to think of it, I don't suppose the disciples would have invented this method. The Christians gained nothing by this particular belief. In fact, they laid themselves open to the charge—forgive the phrase—that Jesus was a bastard. As a matter of history this very allegation was made by the first opponents of Christianity. Yet Christians never withdrew; they continued to assert the fact of Jesus and His virgin birth. They believed it not because they wanted to—but because the facts compelled them to accept it. It was Mary's secret, and she had showed it to them.

For us, it is our faith in Jesus Christ Himself that matters —and not the method of His birth, the way He chose to come among us. Yet I do suggest that the virgin birth seems, just as a key fits into its lock, to fit perfectly into the whole story of God coming in the person of Jesus Christ to deliver man.

Suggested Bible reading: Matthew, chapter 1, verses 18 to 25.

THE HEART OF THE CROSS

THROUGHOUT the centuries since Jesus Christ was crucified the Cross of Calvary has been the supreme symbol of self-sacrifice and suffering love.

Here is a great mystery. God came close to us in Jesus and took our human nature upon Him that He might bring us back into friendship with Himself.

Yet the people of Christ's day did not understand. In their selfishness and blindness they rejected Him so that under Pontius Pilate He was condemned to be crucified. And we would have done just the same had we been among them.

We have no business to blame the Jews or the Romans. What crucified Christ was just ordinary human nature, too selfish and too blind to understand what God wanted, too self-willed to accept God's way. It is this attitude of mind which has always made God to suffer, spurned His goodness, crucified His love.

This is the heart of the mystery of the Cross of Christ. The Cross towers over the passing centuries, and remains always the symbol of how man hurts God, and how God, because He loves us, suffers through our sin and blindness.

If that were all that we could see in the Cross of Calvary, then it would be a condemning fact; but there is something else. It is that God in His amazing love does not repudiate us and reject us, even if we reject Him. He is still willing to forgive—"Father, forgive them, for they know not what they do." He still offers us His friendship, and will, if we let Him, by His Spirit take hold of our lives and make us better people.

No wonder, then, that Christians have always looked up to the Cross of Jesus with penitence and love and gratitude, and have found that as they discover something of the meaning of God's love they themselves begin to know what it means really to be a Christian.

Suggested Bible reading: Romans, chapter 5, verses 1 to 11.

WHY CHRIST CAME BACK

"THE third day He arose again from the dead...."

Every time I say the Creed, I am struck by the challenging and defiant note that rings through this sentence.

Man, by his sin and wilful self-centredness, condemned Christ to the Cross. We—for the men of His time were no different from ourselves; they represent us,—we repudiated His love, turned our backs on His goodness. We thought we could get rid of Him and run our lives without God.

But we couldn't do it. He came back; He came back alive. He came back the triumphant victor over sin and death.

Now He is still with us, always present, the King of mankind.

This is the tremendous and exciting message of Easter. Yes, I mean that word exciting—isn't it exciting?

When we feel lonely, He is there to be our Friend. Frustrated and wondering whether the struggle against evil and pain is worth while, we can be sure of His strength, and even more, know that we can share His victory if we trust Him to help us.

Here is the very hope the sick and weary world to-day needs to know. If only it will respond and return in surrender and trust to the risen Christ of God, then there will be a new release of spiritual power.

I have stated quite simply what the story of Easter has to say to us. I realise that the great difficulty for many people is to believe that it ever happened. Can we really believe that God raised Christ from the dead? We will go on to consider some of the reasons why Christians believe this amazing fact.

But first I want you to realise the hope that Easter offers you and me. Perhaps in the long run the only satisfactory proof that Christ rose from the dead is to know in our hearts and lives that He is our personal and living Saviour.

He is ready to give us this proof if we will welcome Him into our inmost being.

Suggested Bible reading: Philippians, chapter 3, verses 8 to 13.

PROOF POSITIVE

BEFORE considering some of the reasons why Christians have always believed that Jesus Christ rose from the dead on that first Easter Day, let us be quite clear about this: it is possible to be a genuine believer in Jesus Christ without being able to state the evidence for the truth of the Resurrection. Many people live by a simple faith, and it is quite sufficient.

There are, however, others who want to know the reason why. For these there are three main lines of evidence.

After His Resurrection Jesus appeared to a number of people—Peter, John, Mary and Thomas, and to all the disciples together. On another occasion it was to a crowd of some 500; and perhaps most significant of all, he appeared to Paul. Paul was not looking for the risen Christ, remember —he was opposed to the whole business, and was on his way to persecute the Christians in Damascus.

Why should we doubt the evidence of these people, who had nothing to gain by inventing the story, and in fact, were persecuted just because, believing that Christ was risen from the dead, they tried to serve Him and pass on the good news?

In the second place we have the evidence of the empty tomb. True, it could be said that the disciples stole the body; but, then, how can we believe that such people as they would be could foist on the world a deliberate lie? And, if the enemies of Jesus took the body, they would have produced it at once to kill the story of the Resurrection. So the fact of the empty tomb remains.

Finally, and perhaps most important, there is the transformation of the disciples. Peter, for instance, who had denied his Lord, became a man of courage with the power of vigorous leadership. Why? Because he was certain that his master Christ had risen from the dead and was always present with him to give strength and confidence. The same change happened to all the other disciples.

It is for this reason that the Christian Church has believed in the truth of the Resurrection. But to this must be added the fact that throughout the centuries since the Resurrection multitudes of men and women, ordinary people like ourselves, have found in their own experience the presence of the living Christ to reinforce and make absolutely certain the evidence of the first disciples.

Suggested Bible reading: 1 Corinthians, chapter 15, verses 1 to 14.

HE GIVES US COURAGE

IN my series about the Apostles' Creed, you may have noticed that I passed straight from the death of Jesus upon the Cross to His Resurrection, missing out that very puzzling clause, "He descended into hell."

I did this, not because I wanted to avoid a phrase that is difficult, but because I wanted to link closely together the Crucifixion on Calvary with the Resurrection in the Garden.

Now we must go back, and think about this phrase, "He descended into hell."

A puzzled inquirer once reminded me that "Jesus Himself told the dying thief, 'To-day shalt thou be with Me in paradise.' How can these two statements be reconciled?"

Let me say at once that I think the phrase in the Apostles' Creed is unnecessarily difficult for ordinary people. In the English version of the New Testament, two Greek words are both translated "hell." One is "*Gehenna*," which refers to the final state of the utterly wicked; this is the hell of which we generally think and speak.

The other word is "*Hades*," which means the place of the departed spirits, the state in which those who die await the final resurrection. What this state is we do not know, and cannot really understand, but "paradise" is also a term for the place of departed spirits.

Jesus promised the thief that he would be with Him that

day in the place of the departed spirits, to which, when He died, Jesus passed; or, as the Apostles' Creed puts it, "He descended into hell."

This is a comforting thought. Just as during His earthly life Jesus was tempted in all points as we are, yet without sin, so that He can really sympathise and understand our human experiences; so, too, He died a real human death, meeting the fear of the unknown.

To Him we can trust our loved ones when they descend into the place of the departed spirits, sure of His love and understanding. At the time of our death, too, He can give us confidence and courage—dying grace for the hour of dying. "It is I," He will whisper, "be not afraid."

Suggested Bible reading: Luke, chapter 23, verses 39 to 43.

CHRIST IS EVERYWHERE

I ALWAYS find the story of Christ's Ascension into Heaven rather difficult to understand.

The Bible tells us that Jesus, after His Resurrection, met His disciples on a number of occasions, talked with them and taught them; then one day while they were together on the top of a low mountain He suddenly disappeared from their sight, and they saw Him no more, though they never lost the certainty of His spiritual presence.

What exactly happened we do not know, but it may be that a mountain mist enveloped Him, and from that moment He was lost to sight. He never again appeared to His disciples. Or maybe something quite out of the ordinary happened, and Jesus was caught up and disappeared in a cloud. I think the former is more likely.

But in either case the important fact is that the physical presence of Jesus was never again given to His disciples. They were sure that He was back again in the presence of the Eternal God in the heavenly sphere.

We talk about an ascension, or going up, because we find it easier to think of Heaven as above the bright blue sky, though in fact it is a state, not a place.

This, then, is the bare story of the Ascension, and perhaps it doesn't seem nearly so important to us as the events that happened at Christmas, Good Friday and Easter; but it is.

If Jesus had not ascended, and His physical presence had remained with us, we should always be wondering exactly where at any given moment He would be. If we heard He was in America, we would wish He were in England; if in Australia, the African Christians would want Him. Our thoughts would be fixed upon the value of having Him actually present in the flesh.

But what really matters to our religion is that He is always everywhere present by the Spirit. We can never get away from Him; He is in our midst ready to help and to guide.

This abiding conviction that the living Jesus Christ is always with His people is the foundation of the moral and spiritual power of Christianity.

Suggested Bible reading: Colossians, chapter 3, verses 1 to 4.

GOD UNDERSTANDS

I DON'T care for long words—and I'm sure you don't either. "Anthropomorphic" is one of them; but there is no other word that will do, so I must use it.

It means, as you know, "in the likeness of a man," and is

used when we refer to God in words or ideas which we use in connection with men. It doesn't mean that we are trying to make God like ourselves, but that all we can do when we talk about God is to use human words and pictures. These are just pointers to what we are trying to say about God. They are never exact, but they are the best we can do.

This phrase in the Creed is plainly anthropomorphic—"He sitteth on the right hand of God the Father Almighty."

We are trying to say something about Jesus Christ which is very difficult to express. He is truly man, human like ourselves. He died on a Cross, He rose again, He ascended into Heaven; but He is also God, truly God.

Now in Heaven there is in the experience of God, the experience of human living, human temptation, and human suffering.

How can we picture this, that the infinite, almighty and eternal God has within His own nature this experience of human living? We picture it by saying that Jesus Christ, God Incarnate, who took our human nature upon Him, "sitteth on the right hand of the Father Almighty." There, in a position of equal authority and majesty, alongside the Father is the Lord Jesus Christ.

This kind of picture helps us to grasp the fact that God understands and sympathises with our human experience and human difficulties, because He, too, has experienced them. He is not a remote and distant God. As we pray to Him we can, as it were, see Jesus Christ who lived here on earth with us, reigning in Heaven as our Lord and Saviour.

This gives us confidence in our approach to God, and makes us quite sure not only that He understands but that Manhood has been taken up to the Throne of God.

Suggested Bible reading: Hebrews, chapter 7, verses 24 to 28.

GOD HATES ALL EVIL

THE H-bomb has shocked all thinking people. It couldn't be otherwise when we remember the appalling progress we have made in the art of destroying each other.

Within forty years we have had poison gas, saturation bombing, the atom bomb, and now this last unthinkable horror. Mankind has never been more clever, and at the same time never more inventive in ways of mass murder.

If there is a good God, how can man hope to get away with such evil? If this is a moral world, then there must be a judgment, somewhere, sometime, somehow.

Yet it is all too easy to feel this about great evils, and to forget that small sins also deserve God's judgment. After all, the basic flaws in human nature—aggressiveness, selfishness, jealousy, dishonesty, and all ungodliness—are the material out of which large international evils are fashioned.

We can't believe that God is indifferent to this kind of behaviour. Jesus Christ showed us God's love, yes indeed—but He also showed us that God is utterly good, and hates all evil.

It may appear for a moment as if evil seems to be successful, and that those who do wrong can get away with it; but it is not true in the long run. The Creed declares, "He shall come to judge the quick and the dead."

Not only in this life do we suffer if we do wrong. The Bible declares that at the end there will be some kind of decisive judgment.

Exactly what it means, or what it may be like, we do not know, but we may be certain that all of us will have to face the fact of the goodness of God, and of His judgment upon sin.

Some people may be influenced to turn from sin by the thought of future judgment, and to hand over their lives to the service of Christ.

I think perhaps we have forgotten this element of fear in much of our religious thinking to-day. Whether we turn to Christ through fear or through love, it is certain that only when with genuine repentance we seek God's forgiveness can we be released from the dread of God's judgment and be confident that in spite of our sins we can live as His forgiven children, both here and hereafter.

Suggested Bible reading: Hebrews, chapter 9, verses 23 to 28.

HE LONGS TO HELP US

I suppose that what Christians value most about their religion is the knowledge that the presence of the living Christ is always with them.

Yet they do not think of this presence as if He were standing by them. They are certain that He is within them.

> Speak to Him thou, for He hears,
> And Spirit with spirit can meet;
> Closer is He than breathing,
> Nearer than hands and feet.

This is what we mean when we say that the Holy Spirit dwells within us. We commemorate His first coming into the hearts and lives of men on Whit Sunday; and we proclaim this glad truth in the Creed when we say, "I believe in the Holy Ghost."

It is rather a wonderful fact, when you come to think of it. God, the great Spirit behind the Universe, has shown us something of His goodness and love in Jesus Christ. This Jesus, having died for our sins, has conquered evil and death.

Now, as the living Holy Spirit, He comes back into the personalities of those who will receive Him, so that they may have the power to live as His children, and to bring forth in their lives something of His likeness.

It was this coming of the Holy Spirit that transformed those first disciples, and made them, weak and sinful though they were, into such mighty soldiers for the cause of Christ.

It is the same Holy Spirit who ever since in countless thousands of lives has worked the same miracle.

Jesus said, when He was on earth: "How much more shall your Heavenly Father give the Holy Spirit to them that ask Him." The promise still holds good.

Anyone to-day who is weak, frustrated, conscious of sin and shame, yet wants to be better—anyone like this, or with any other personal problem or spiritual need, can come, and in a simple prayer of faith ask for and claim the gift of the Holy Spirit.

Such a simple, honest asking for God to take possession of our lives is all that God waits for. In His love He longs to help us; by our free will we can either accept that help or refuse it.

Suggested Bible reading: Luke, chapter 11, verses 1 to 13.

ONE FOLD, ONE SHEPHERD

ONE of the most common criticisms directed against Christianity is that Christians are divided.

"Look at you," says the critic, "you all profess to follow one Master, so why can't you all belong to one Church? Instead there are Roman Catholics, Protestants, Eastern Orthodox and hundreds of smaller groups calling themselves Christians. It doesn't make sense to me."

It didn't make sense either to our Lord Himself. He quite clearly says that His purpose is that we may all be one— "One fold, one shepherd."

So it was at the very beginning. If you were a Christian, then you were a member of the Christian Church, and there was just one Christian Church.

It was a "holy" Church. This doesn't mean that Christians were perfect—of course not, for they had their failures and their sins; but they were trying to follow Christ.

The Church itself as a body had imperfections and made mistakes; but it was "set apart"—that is what "holy" really means—for the worship, witness and work of Christ.

It was also "Catholic." The word means "universal," and throughout the civilised world in those early days there were branches of the Christian Church, and each branch felt a common loyalty to the other branches.

But to-day, unfortunately, we are divided into different sections and different churches. This is a great sin, and all of us who love Jesus Christ should pray and work to re-establish unity amongst all Christians.

We are, of course, partially united already in so far as we love and serve the same Master. We need not criticise each other; we are working for the same cause; we have many beliefs in common, and can co-operate, if we want to, in Christian enterprises.

For instance, here in Birmingham, Roman Catholics and Protestants have united in showing a religious film, *I Beheld His Glory*, to interest non-churchgoers in the message of the Gospel.

But this unity of spirit is not enough. We must pray that

the day will come when there will be one visible Church of Christ to which all men will look when they turn their eyes towards the Christian Faith.

Suggested Bible reading: John, chapter 10, verses 7 to 16.

WE ARE ALL HIS PEOPLE

SOMETIMES I lecture on "Love and Marriage." It is always difficult to find words to describe what real love is, but when I try to do so, it is very interesting to watch the audience.

Here and there you will see people who show by the look in their eyes and the animation of their faces that they are trying, as it were, to say to me, "I don't think you are explaining it very well. I would do it very differently; but I *know* what you mean. You love, and I love. We share the same experience."

So it is when I talk about Jesus Christ, the meaning of His love, the wonder of His forgiveness and the reality of His friendship. People's eyes sparkle; you can see by their smile that they know what I am talking about. We share the same experience.

This is true of all Christians everywhere, no matter to which Church we belong, no matter what race or language is our's, no matter how we became real Christians. We are all at one in this: we are in Christ, and His Spirit dwells in our hearts. We share the same experience.

This is what we mean when we say, "I believe in the communion of saints." We assert that all the world over, without regard to nationality, colour, intellect, position, wealth or anything else, all real Christians belong to one family, and are united in spirit with each other.

But we mean more than this. Because we believe that when we die the believer in Christ joins the fellowship of the blessed dead—who are not really dead, but are, through Christ, living in God's nearer presence—we are sure that our fellowship as Christians is unbroken. We are one not only with all Christians on the earth; but we are also one with those Christians who have gone on before through death to the fuller life.

We hope that they pray for us; we certainly can remember them with gratitude and thanksgiving. We do not know much about their state, but we are confident that the same Heavenly Father who looks after them looks after us. We are all His redeemed people, and for ever bound to Him in love and loyalty.

Suggested Bible reading: Ephesians, chapter 2, verses 11 to 22.

FRIENDS WITH GOD

MANY people seem to me to be muddled about the idea of the forgiveness of sins. "Why do I need to be forgiven? And how can I go on again and again asking to be forgiven for the same sins?"

I see the difficulties here, but they aren't as real as they sound. All of us, at any rate from time to time, know perfectly well that we have sinned and done wrong; we feel guilty and ashamed, and wish we could get rid of the burden of the wrongdoing.

What is hard when we feel like this is to grasp the fact it is God's forgiveness that we need. God is so often rather unreal and distant that it makes it hard for us to feel that we have sinned against Him.

It is only, I think, as God becomes more real to us through Christ that we can more consciously know that we need His forgiveness.

The other difficulty is simpler. There is a forgiveness which is once and for all. I receive it when I come to God with genuine sincerity and determination, and I ask Him to forgive me, to put me into a new relationship with Himself, a relationship of friendship.

This restoration to a right relationship with God is meant to be once for all, permanent, just as there is a relationship with one's wife or husband which is permanent and decisive.

Day by day, however, I shall, alas!, fail in many respects to please God and do His will. For these faults and misdemeanours I must tell him I am sorry, so that the evil will not accumulate and spoil our relationship.

Here, too, the marriage analogy applies. Often we have to say we are sorry to one whose relationship of love with us is quite unbroken by our faults; none the less, we need to ask for pardon, otherwise small faults may accumulate into an awkward barrier.

All this is what we mean when we say, "I believe in the forgiveness of sins." It is offered to us simply because God loves us, and in Jesus Christ He has shown His love unmistakably.

Suggested Bible reading: 1 John, chapter 1, verses 1 to 9.

IN CHRIST WE SHALL LIVE FOR EVER

GREAT changes have been taking place in the parish of St. Martin's-in-the-Bull Ring. The citizens responded marvellously to the recent appeal for £100,000 to restore the parish church of Birmingham. I was most grateful.

We have started to use the money, and some of the work put in hand has been to excavate part of the old churchyard in order to lay the foundations of a new hall adjoining the church.

We are discovering bones and skulls of people buried hundreds of years ago on this site. They will be re-buried with a simple prayer in a neighbouring cemetery.

What has interested me are the comments of the ordinary folk who know what is happening. Many of them, I find, really think that at the Resurrection Day the particles of their old human body will miraculously come together again, and link up, as it were, with their soul.

I suppose they are puzzled by the phrase, "I believe in the resurrection of the body."

In the first Epistle to the Corinthians, chapter 15, St. Paul tells us the truth about this great and glorious fact. When we die, he says, our natural body will be buried, and I think from this we can infer decay. At the Resurrection each personality, each soul, will be raised by the power of God, and clothed in a "spiritual body." These are Paul's actual words.

He is telling us that we shall not live on in the Resurrection life as disembodied souls, but as real individual personalities in spiritual form. Whether we take on the likeness of our old body in any degree we can't tell, but the great truth is that we still shall be our true selves—our best selves, purified from sin, and therefore from the possibility of suffering and decay.

In Christ we shall live for ever as full and perfect spiritual beings.

Suggested Bible reading: 1 Corinthians, chapter 15.

LIFE EVERLASTING

The Apostles' Creed ends with a phrase full of confidence and hope. "I believe in the life everlasting."

We must not think from this that the be-all and end-all of Christianity is Heaven when we die; or, as a heckler in the open air often puts it, "Pie in the sky when we die." Christianity certainly isn't "Pie to-morrow, but never pie to-day."

Life everlasting means real life, that deep, inner spiritual life of fellowship with God which is man's true riches. It is this that God means man really to have and to enjoy, for God made us for fellowship with Himself.

This personal relationship with God through Jesus Christ, this inner real spiritual life, while it expresses itself through the body here and now on earth, is the kind of life which physical death cannot possibly destroy. After death this life in Christ will still be ours.

So the Christian faith offers a life of spiritual vitality and purpose here on this earth, and because of its vitality, real practical changes in society as well as in individual lives; and for these changes there is a great deal of evidence, if we look back over the history of the last two thousand years.

Christianity also offers beyond this world, and at the end of history, a continued life in fellowship with God for ever.

In this hope Christians have lived and died; and it is this message which Christians seek to share with their fellow men. There is nothing narrow or merely pious in this virile faith. It is a hope which enables man to face life as he finds it here and now, and to face it in a Christian spirit. It is a hope which gives him a power to overcome some of its evil and suffering and to try to redeem the society in which he lives and to build a better world. Then in this same hope he can look beyond and see a purpose for man in a life free from sin and sorrow in perfect fellowship with God, the Creator and Father of all mankind.

Suggested Bible reading: Revelation, chapter 21, verse 22 to chapter 22, verse 5.

II
THE WAY OF THE KINGDOM

A WORLD-FAMOUS SERMON

WHEN you were last at a baby's baptism in church, I wonder if you noticed a rather strange phrase? Right at the end of the service the parents and godparents are told to bring the baby to church in order to "hear sermons"—as it is quaintly phrased in the English Book of Common Prayer.

Poor innocent little creature, what a thought—to be taken "to hear sermons"!

I know some sermons are good, but plenty of them are bad. Or rather, over our heads and a bit dull.

There is, however, one world-famous sermon of which everybody has heard—the sermon preached by Jesus Christ to the crowds that gathered round him on a hillside by the Sea of Galilee, which we call the Sermon on the Mount.

It has exercised a quite remarkable influence on the thought of the world. Many people who would not call themselves Christians or, in fact, who would go even further and deny Christianity altogether, do accept the sublime teaching of this Sermon.

The interesting question has been raised whether the teaching was all given at the same time, or whether the writer of Matthew's Gospel has collected together in the famous 5th, 6th, and 7th chapters scattered sayings and teachings of Our Lord, and put them together in the form of a continuous discourse.

I don't think it really matters which is the right answer.

In these chapters we have the sort of thing that Jesus Christ was always preaching and teaching, so that we are listening here, as we read, to what Jesus Christ wants to say to His disciples.

Suggested Bible reading: Matthew, chapters 5, 6 and 7.

THE BLESSED LIFE

THE most famous section of the Sermon on the Mount is the Beatitudes, those nine wonderful sayings at the beginning of the fifth chapter of St. Matthew's Gospel. "Blessed are the poor in spirit, for theirs is the Kingdom of Heaven"—and then follow eight more declarations of Jesus concerning the way to live happily.

Amongst our friends we often refer to "so and so" as a "good type." In this passage, Jesus outlines the "Christian type." He describes the way a person should live, or rather should try to live, who wants to be a good disciple of His, or a sound member of His Kingdom.

Two points strike me at once as I read the Beatitudes. I realise, first of all, that by "blessed" Jesus does not mean happy in a trivial, superficial kind of way.

He is referring to that deep, inner contentment and happiness of heart which no passing troubles or even quite deep sorrows can touch. He means a sound, purposeful and true kind of life.

I remember once seeing a very fine picture. There was a rock amid a wild, raging gale. The stormy sea was dashing ceaselessly against it; white spray was being blown up into the skies. It was a scene of strife, restlessness, storm—fearful and awe-inspiring.

But there, in a crevice in the rock, quietly sleeping, was a seagull, at rest in the storm—at peace amid the turmoil.

That is symbolic of what Jesus means by a "blessed" life. He is not promising an escape from all the rough seas that we all have to encounter if we really are alive; but He is saying there is a blessedness that a man can discover which will keep him in perfect peace amid it all.

Suggested Bible reading: Matthew, chapter 5, verses 3 to 12.

FREE FOR ALL

THE religion of Jesus is free for all. He has no favourites and no one is debarred from discovering the happiness His way of life offers.

One of the striking things about the "blessedness" or happiness about which Jesus talks in the Beatitudes is that it is open for anyone to discover.

How different Jesus is from any other teacher. Aristotle, the Greek philosopher, taught that the happy life was open only to certain classes of people; it was not for slaves, for the diseased, for the dying, or for the young. What a horrible kind of religion!

Buddha said you can't find happiness unless you get rid of your own self—not merely your sinful self, but of the things that make real human life interesting. Only if we empty ourselves of all worldly desire of body and mind, shall we find true happiness and put in its place heavenly desire.

Others have taught that we must avoid pain and suffering and shrink from humiliation, and then, if we are lucky, we will be happy.

But not so with Jesus. In the Beatitudes He urges us actively to meet life, giving ourselves to it—but in the right way.

If a man does this, keeping his eyes fixed on what is really worth aiming at, and then trying to achieve it, he will find, not necessarily material success, but in spiritual character a personal life which is really "blessed," which really wins a respect from his fellow men—and above all, is approved by God.

Suggested Bible reading: Matthew, chapter 5, verses 3 to 12.

PURE IN HEART

"BLESSED are the poor in spirit." Jesus does not mean that we are to be without spirit or personality. He wants us not to be conceited about our spiritual attainments, but to be humble and willing always to receive anything that life teaches.

Mourning and sorrow cannot be avoided; only through such lessons shall we discover the true comfort which comes from realising that pain and death are not the final end; but they are the means for achieving a spiritual triumph at the end.

How young people dislike the phrase "Blessed are the meek!" That is because they think Jesus suggests that we should be "door-mats." He simply warns us against being self-assertive and proud.

How right He is! Hitler and the Nazis were self-assertive, and they did not inherit the earth.

Men, says Jesus, hunger and thirst after money, popularity and power, and the more they strain the more dissatisfied they often are, but if, He says, you "hunger and thirst after righteousness," you will find that being good and doing good is always satisfying.

If we show mercy, we shall receive mercy. This is one of my own personal experiences; I have found it so.

"The pure in heart." Jesus is not referring simply to

sexual decency of act and thought. He means that only people who are sincere and open will ever really see God. Spiritual discoveries are never made by the dishonest, the hypocritical or the prejudiced.

Then Jesus moves to a climax. If you really want to be a child with a character like your Father God, then, He says, be a peacemaker. For God in His love is always seeking to make us right with Himself and to give us the peace of His forgiveness; and He wants us to be at peace with each other.

Suggested Bible reading: Matthew, chapter 5, verses 3 to 12.

SALT OF THE EARTH

IN the Sermon on the Mount, Jesus is speaking to His disciples—to people who have professed their desire to follow Him. He is not really speaking to the man in the street.

This is rather important, I think, if we are to understand the teaching of Jesus. We cannot take some of the ideas in this Sermon and apply them to a non-Christian society; we cannot impose them on a secular state.

The fact is that Christ is giving guidance for the personal behaviour of Christians who are already within the brotherhood of a conscious discipleship to Himself.

Before we can obey the Sermon we must accept the Saviour and Sovereign Lord as the Master of our lives. Jesus always made this perfectly clear—that if a man wants to be a Christian he must first give personal love and trust to Christ himself.

What a remarkable privilege Jesus considered discipleship

to be. He says, for instance, about His followers that they are the "salt of the earth."

Our idea of salt is that food unsalted is horribly tasteless and not worth eating. This is certainly true, but there is another idea about salt: it is the great preservative which keeps materials from decaying. Christianity has been one of the greatest morally progressive, spiritual forces in the world.

You can always recognise salt. It gives the food a distinctive flavour. How tragic it is that sometimes Christians have lost this distinctiveness. You cannot tell that they are present in a home, in a street, in a factory or in a club. We should be able to do so, for they should be giving a clear, distinctive witness by the way they live and the way they speak.

Suggested Bible reading: Matthew, chapter 5, verse 13.

LIGHT OF THE WORLD

GREECE, in her time, was the mother of some of the world's greatest men.

What a golden age it was!

Think of them: Socrates, one of the world's great philosophers; Plato, his disciple—and another, Thucydides, a historian whose fame will never cease; Sophocles, Euripides, Aeschylus, great and renowned poets, and Phidias, the amazing sculptor whose Parthenon in Athens to-day is the admiration of the world.

These were some of the great lights of ancient Greece, and their insights and achievements have shone like beacons in our world.

In the Sermon on the Mount, Jesus says His disciples are

to be like that: shining like lights in the world, though their light is not necessarily to be the achievement of dramatic art, or of architect's skill, or of poetic genius.

They are to be known by the purity and integrity of their lives.

The light of character, as Jesus points out, cannot be hid, and it is not meant to be.

When we light a candle we don't put a cover on it, we put it on a candle-stick where everybody can benefit from its light.

So, says Jesus, "Let your light so shine before men that they may see your good works and glorify your Father Which is in Heaven."

We must not think as we read these words of Jesus that He is summoning His disciples to a great effort of light-shining. What He is asking for is a simple-hearted, humble trust in Himself, for a daily following in His footsteps.

So, He says, such people will unconsciously be shining lights which nobody can fail to notice.

Plato has a striking phrase in his *Republic*—"Those having torches will pass them on to others." The Christian who shines with the goodness of God will influence society.

Suggested Bible reading: Matthew, chapter 5, verses 14 to 16.

THE KINGDOM OF LOVE

SOME people have said that Jesus was rather too hard on the Scribes and Pharisees. After all, they were very religious, punctilious about their prayers and most scrupulous in keeping the Commandments.

Yet, in the Sermon on the Mount, Jesus says, "Except

BEING AND BELIEVING

your righteousness exceed the righteousness of the Scribes and Pharisees, ye shall in no way enter the Kingdom of Heaven."

What does He mean? What was wrong with the Pharisees was that they were tied by "red tape" in their standards of behaviour. As long as the correct thing was done outwardly, the motive and spirit did not matter.

To Jesus this was an anathema. Of course, it is easier to be given a set of rules. Then if you observe them in the letter, you can say to yourself, "Well done; I'm not so bad after all."

But to give a man some principles and a general spirit by which he is supposed to live is not nearly so easy—but much better.

Now suppose, before I went off to Australia, my wife had said to me, "Bryan, here are ten rules for your behaviour while you are away. Keep them."

Perhaps, if I tried very hard, I should be able to keep them; then when I came back I should be able to say, "See how good I have been."

But she did not give me any rules at all.

She just allowed me to go, believing that I should want to please her and do what I know she would want me to do. So I had to behave in the right spirit, according to her desires.

That made me think; it gave me liberty, and yet really it was much more binding because of the love in our relationship.

That is why Jesus says that the righteousness of His disciples must exceed that of the Pharisees. His Kingdom is a kingdom of love, and it is by loving God and trying to please Him that we fulfil the law of Christ.

Suggested Bible reading: Matthew, chapter 5, verses 17 to 20.

BE FRIENDS FIRST

UNDER the Jewish law, the *act* of murder was punishable. In the Sermon on the Mount, Jesus raised the whole standard of guilt.

"Whosoever is angry with his brother," He cries, "shall be in danger of judgment." Malicious anger is out of place in the life of one of His disciples.

Speaking metaphorically, He warns us against cursing people—and saying, "Thou fool." We must not take Him literally here, but the spirit of His injunction is right. Violent anger and abuse of others are unbecoming to those who profess to be the disciples of Christ.

But, as usual, Jesus is not merely negative: He always gives positive instructions.

He goes on to tell us that it should be our business to remove grievances before letting them lead to anger, to pay our debts and to go out of our way to get rid of causes of bitterness and malice.

How can you possibly go to church to offer the gift of your worship to God before the altar, when you have quarrelled with a relative or the next-door neighbour?

Be friends first, and then go to worship God afterwards. This statement hits us straight between the eyes.

Both in church and outside it, there is far too much jealousy, bitterness and quarrelling, and surprisingly, we often refuse to put things right.

I well remember, some years ago, a middle-aged lady telling me with great bitterness that she had not spoken to her sister for twenty years.

Some grievance, imaginary or otherwise, had built up a wall which neither of them was willing to break down.

"I won't forgive her!" she cried angrily to me. "So it is no use your talking."

"Well, madam," I replied, "then God won't forgive you, so it is no use your asking Him."

Suggested Bible reading: Matthew, chapter 5, verses 21 to 26.

LIVE AS A CHILD OF GOD

IN some circles, both in church and outside, there appear to be only four sins that really matter—murder, adultery, lying, and stealing.

I always feel this is probably because the people who think like this are quite sure they have never committed any of the four—and are therefore quite complacent and sure that they at least are good!

Jesus hated this kind of self-complacency and torpedoed it in His famous Sermon on the Mount. Adultery, He reminded His hearers, was not simply an act of taking another man's wife.

He pointed out that trying to steal her love without touching her body is adultery.

He went even further, and said that the sin is really committed if a man allows himself in his heart to plan and contrive to win the affection of somebody else to whom he has no right—or allows such a deep desire to grow in his thoughts.

Here, you see, Jesus is putting the emphasis on motive and inward thinking, and not simply on the outward act.

He takes the same line about divorce. In His day there was a rule by which a man could get rid of his wife simply by an outward act of writing a notice saying that he divorced her.

You cannot do that, says Jesus. She really belongs to her

husband, and is part of him. That is the true nature of marriage. They are one flesh and one spirit. Divorce therefore is a more serious matter than a simple, formal renunciation. If what matters in the eyes of Jesus is motive and desire, then self-discipline is necessary—and that is never easy.

To drive home His point Jesus uses a most striking metaphor. He says, "If thy right hand offend thee, cut it off, for it is profitable for thee that one of thy members should perish, and not that thy whole body should be cast into Hell."

At all costs, we must control our bodies and minds. Man's great dignity is when he lives not as a creature of animal instincts but as master of his own soul, as a child of his Heavenly Father.

Suggested Bible reading: Matthew, chapter 5, verses 27 to 32.

RAISE THE STANDARD

THE people in the days of Jesus made a great use of oaths. The Jews solemnly put themselves in the Presence of God and then made a statement.

On ordinary occasions, however, they were not nearly so particular about keeping promises or telling lies.

Jesus sweeps aside all this casuistry for His disciples. Everything we say ought to be true; all our promises must be kept. A hallmark of Christians should be straightforward honesty.

In His teaching about this in the Sermon on the Mount, Jesus points out that the Jewish attitude was wrong because it was at heart blasphemous.

We cannot put ourselves in the Presence of God—we are always there; He knows what we say and what we promise.

Therefore, we must keep our promises and speak the truth.

What a challenge this is to us to-day! Nations and governments, individuals and groups, seem to have lost the simple integrity where "yes" means yes and "no" means no.

What is worse, we excuse ourselves and say it is difficult or impossible to keep a promise, so we must break it; it is too hard to tell the truth, so we tell a white lie.

An interesting point, which some Christians have thought important, is raised by this passage. If Jesus says that our simple word ought to be enough, is it necessary to swear an oath when giving evidence in a police court?

Strictly, I don't think it ought to be. But because at this stage of civilisation there is so much evil in the world, it is probably a wise additional precaution.

If the whole standard of integrity were higher, then such oaths as this would become quite unnecessary. The business of Christians is to raise the standard.

Suggested Bible reading: Matthew, chapter 5, verses 33 to 37.

TIT FOR TAT

"Tit for tat," and that seems fair; may be; but it isn't Christian. Jesus makes this clear in the Sermon on the Mount, when He points out that the old Law of Moses allowed an eye for an eye and a tooth for a tooth.

A man could revenge himself up to the point of exact reciprocity.

Now, that wasn't altogether bad. A savage rushes blindly in, when he is hurt, to do as much damage as possible. So the old law limits human instincts.

Jesus required more than this from His disciples. He wants self-effacement and the complete control of our personal feelings.

Listen to His classic remark, "Whosoever shall smite thee on thy right cheek, turn to him the other also."

Don't say it is too hard or it cannot be done. Although perhaps we are not meant to take this saying of Jesus literally, we *are* meant to apply it thoughtfully to the various situations that arise in our own personal lives.

Let me explain. Jesus is speaking in proverbs; proverbs are not literal precepts of behaviour, because often they are contradictory.

Take, for instance, "Look before you leap," then I shall quote the opposite—"Nothing venture nothing have."

Or, "Penny wise, pound foolish"; in contrast, "Take care of the pence, and the pounds will take care of themselves."

In each of these proverbs there is a germ of truth which we must apply as the occasion arises.

So with this teaching of Jesus. We must not constantly be thinking of our own rights. We must be willing to sacrifice our own feelings, and not take revenge, and so create more trouble.

Forgiving love, and a generous attitude to those who hurt us, make all the difference to the way the wheels of the world go round.

What a wretched business human society would be—in fact, often is—except on these principles of restraint and generosity which Jesus urges.

Suggested Bible reading: Matthew, chapter 5, verses 38 to 42.

BE FRIENDS WITH YOUR FOES

It is easy to be nice to people we like; but to those we hate, it is very hard. Yet Jesus says in the Sermon on the Mount, "Love your enemies."

We say, "That's impossible," and so disregard His teaching. It is obvious that we cannot like everyone equally.

But if we want to be good disciples of Jesus we must have the attitude of love towards everybody, and be willing to give them the best we have.

God redeems men by treating them not as they are, but as they are capable of becoming. That is why we must not treat our personal enemies as implacable foes who will never alter, but as people who could become friends if we treat them properly and if they are willing to respond.

Nobody pretends that this is easy, and no doubt there are circumstances in which we just cannot carry out this teaching completely. That is true in the case of war, when the whole of society is involved, and not just individuals.

But we must take the principle that Jesus outlines here quite seriously—we can all carry it out better than we do.

When you come to think of it, Jesus is utterly reasonable. If our Heavenly Father gives His good gifts of Nature and His loving help to all men the world over, whether they believe in Him and try to obey Him or whether they don't, we ought to do the same.

We must try to be friends with foreigners, with uncongenial people, with those who criticise us. To the real Christian all barriers of race and class must disappear.

We are all children of the same Father, and mere differences of temperament, taste, culture or colour should not prevent us from being friends.

This attitude is the only way in which we can attempt to be the kind of people that God wants. If we want to be "perfect" disciples, this is the way we must behave.

Suggested Bible reading: Matthew, chapter 5, verses 43 to 48.

MONEY IS A TRUST

THE other day I had a good chuckle. I saw a fellow and his girl coming out of the Post Office. Outside was a beggar selling rather inferior shoe-laces. He asked the fellow to buy some. From where I stood I could see he was about to refuse. But the girl was with him. I could almost read his thoughts—"Will she think me mean if I pass this beggar by?" So he stopped and bought some of the shoe-laces.

What was the value of his kindness or charity? In the eyes of Jesus, none, for he only did it to obtain the approval of his girl, not because he wanted to help the man.

On a larger scale some wealthy people only give subscriptions because they want to see their names in the lists and be thought generous by their fellows. To Jesus this is anathema.

Do you remember His words in the Sermon on the Mount? "Take heed that ye do not give your alms before men to be seen of them." Alms-giving—and this is not just putting a penny on the plate in church—is part of a Christian's duty.

Money is a trust, and whether we have much or little, God holds us responsible for the way we spend it.

Some of it is taken from us, whether we like it or not, by a benevolent Government; some we need for the necessities of life.

Some we quite rightly spend on the simple pleasures and extras which are part of man's good living; and some we save, for thrift is a virtue. But there must be a part which we put aside to give generously to those in need, or to help the work of the Christian Church.

The Christian disciple will take trouble to think out how much he gives away; how much he spends, say, on cigarettes or cosmetics, and how much is freely given to help some worthy object.

God knows what we are doing with our money and, according to Jesus, He regards the way we spend it as a test of our true character.

Suggested Bible reading: Matthew, chapter 6, verses 1 to 4.

DO YOU TALK WITH GOD

"I DON'T like the Anglican Prayer Book; it keeps on repeating the same phrase." My critic followed up her first remark by adding, "And Jesus says in the Sermon on the Mount that when we pray we must not use 'vain repetitions.'"

Well, I do like the Prayer Book, and yet I must agree that we are told not to use vain repetitions. The misunderstanding here is due to a wrong interpretation of the words of Jesus.

He was warning us against the heathen practice of thinking there was value in just *saying* prayers without bothering about the words or their meaning.

In Tibet, a Buddhist often takes a piece of paper, writes on it some mysterious or meaningless word. Then, to save himself the trouble of saying the word hundreds of times to obtain some blessing, he puts the paper on a water-wheel and lets the stream turn it, and say the prayer for him.

It is such meaningless talking to God without thought that Jesus condemns.

When we pray we must take trouble about it. We must get alone, as Jesus says, and shut our own door if we want to do business with God through praying. Or we can go into church and find quiet there, either alone or with others.

Such definite concern when we speak to God helps to make prayer real.

Then we must remember that, according to Jesus, our Father knows what we need before we ask Him.

So Christian prayer is not, as it were, bargaining with God, or by much speaking trying to persuade Him to listen and say yes.

It is rather the private, personal talk of a child with a loving Father. We discuss the situation with Him and try to understand His will about it, telling Him how we feel and what we long for.

Such prayer has a real power; only don't forget, as Jesus makes clear, we cannot pray like this if we have sinned and not asked forgiveness—and we cannot ask God's forgiveness if we are not willing to forgive our fellow men.

Suggested Bible reading: Matthew, chapter 6, verses 5 to 15.

HOW TO BE GOOD

> Little Jack Horner
> Sat in the corner
> Eating his Christmas pie;
> He put in his thumb
> And pulled out a plum
> And said, "What a good boy am I."

I SUPPOSE that was either because he didn't gobble up the plum or else had not made himself sick—anyhow, he wanted everybody to know how good he was.

In this he is like many grown-up people. Church people and non-Church people are alike in this. We enjoy advertising the good things we do. We like people to admire us.

Up to a point this can be all right, but often it is very nauseating. It is particularly offensive when people like to show us how religious they are and air their pious deeds in front of our eyes.

How Jesus disliked such people and disapproved of their behaviour! In the Sermon on the Mount, you remember, He told His disciples to behave quite differently.

If they decided to fast—that is, to practice some act of self-denial in order to gain self-discipline—he told them not to parade it like Jack Horners and show everybody what an effort it had been to fast.

Rather, said Jesus, His disciples should be bright and cheerful and disguise the fact that they are practising any self-denial. It is nobody else's business anyhow.

God in Heaven knows and, after all, He will be pleased, and the reward will be a private one, the spiritual reward of a strong character and increased self-discipline.

The Christian disciple should resolutely set his face

against all ostentation, pretence, or show. Like his Master, he should be simple and unassuming, utterly loyal to his convictions, constant in practising his religion, and full of joy.

Suggested Bible reading: Matthew, chapter 6, verses 16 to 18.

SINGLENESS OF PURPOSE

I HAVE recently returned from a most interesting visit to Kenya. One of the things that most impressed my wife and me was the courage of many of the Kikuyu African Christians in the face of Mau Mau terrorism.

We talked to a number of them. I can see one African teacher now as he told me his story.

Day after day, week after week he left the camp where he and others lived under police protection to cycle eight miles to his school. He taught the children, and then cycled back along that lonely road. He had refused to take the Mau Mau oath. He knew the terrorists were after him.

Two other teachers cycling that road were killed, but still he cycled backwards and forwards.

Simply, he told me that he did it because of his love for Jesus Christ, and because it was his duty to teach the children committed to his charge.

Such single-mindedness humbled me. Devotion and enthusiasm like that are very rare.

In the Sermon on the Mount Jesus commended this kind of attitude. He pointed out that if we really love Him, and His service is our greatest "treasure," then our eyes will be fixed on a single goal, and our aim will be to please Him.

This singleness of purpose, this devotion to God, will give meaning and colour to the whole of our life. If we lack this single-mindedness, then no matter what we profess, and no matter what outward churchgoing we practise, our life cannot be and will not be truly Christian.

Suggested Bible reading: Matthew, chapter 6, verses 19 to 23.

SERVING ONE MASTER

I AM in favour of mission preaching like that of Billy Graham, though I don't agree with everything that is said. I think too often the impression is given that it is easy to be a Christian.

In one way, of course, it is; for God offers to us His forgiveness and His friendship, and it is always easy to accept a gift if it is just what we really need. But, from another point of view, to be a Christian is one of the hardest things in the world.

Jesus said quite plainly, "No man can serve two masters. . . . Ye cannot serve God and mammon." That is a quite uncompromising claim which admits of no evasion. We either put God first, or we put ourselves and our interests before Him.

By "mammon" I think Jesus was referring to human society organised in such a way as to leave God out, or to an individual life given over to seeking material good things without any thought of spiritual values. Only one thing can be first in our lives at one time—either God is first, or something else is.

During my recent visit to Africa I came across a certain amount of polygamy, and I found that in a polygamous marriage one of the wives is always a favourite wife, and is recognised as such. Apparently a man can't have two absolutely equal wives. He really loves one better, and she has more influence on him.

So we either have God's interests first, and want to love Christ more than anything, or something or someone else really occupies the centre of our lives.

This demand of Jesus Christ is perfectly reasonable. God, if He is to be God to us at all, must claim our total allegiance. To give Him this allegiance is not easy.

The more one thinks about it, the more frightening it seems, until we remember that in His love God looks at the desire that we have, and not simply at our achievement. If He knows that we want to put Him first, then He accepts that.

Perhaps the greatest wonder of His love is that He accepts us knowing that we shall fail Him, again and again.

This is one of the reasons why the true Christian is so grateful to God.

Suggested Bible reading: Matthew, chapter 6, verse 24; 1 John, chapter 2, verses 15 to 17.

GOD KNOWS OUR NEEDS

I HAVE never been in the position where I have not known where my next meal was coming from, nor have I been without proper clothes or a home.

Other people have, and it is not seemly for those of us who have never experienced such privations to give advice to those who have. Jesus Christ can, and does do so, however.

Simply, and without argument, He states the basic truth in which He believes with all His heart: "Your Heavenly Father knoweth that ye have need of all these things."

To Jesus, God was a loving Father and if He knew His

children needed something desperately then He would provide—that was the faith of Jesus.

And you can't say, "Well, that's all right for Jesus, but it doesn't apply to me," for Jesus tells us that it does.

He says: "Don't have anxious thought about your food and your clothing, for God will look after you just as He looks after the birds of the air and the flowers of the field."

Can we trust God in this simply childlike way that Jesus advises? I don't know what you think as you read these words that I am writing, but I know that I find it very hard to trust God as simply and as steadfastly as this: but we ought to.

Only we must not forget that Jesus does lay down one condition for this loving provision of our Heavenly Father. He reminds us that in our hearts we must seek first God's Kingdom and God's righteousness.

That is to say, He tells us that we must want to live our lives for God and for His glory, and we must be willing to do what is right and what we know will please God—then, and only then, can we be certain that our Heavenly Father will care for us, and that all these things that we need will be given to us.

Suggested Bible reading: Matthew, chapter 6, verses 25 to 34.

SEARCH YOUR OWN MOTIVES

"Judge not, that ye be not judged." Do these words of Jesus mean that a Christian mustn't make estimates of other people's characters—mustn't decide whether a man is honest or not, and so forth?

I don't think these words have anything whatever to do

with a reasonable discernment about people. What Jesus is forbidding among His disciples is a critical attitude which is always looking out for faults in other people. A harsh, fault-finding attitude which always thinks the worst—that, He says, isn't becoming in those who follow Him.

How true this is! We all know people who seem to forget altogether their own faults and shortcomings, and yet think hardly and speak harshly of other people.

Jesus warns us that if this is our way of thinking and speaking it will come back on us in the end.

Life is a strange yet impartial kind of referee. I fancy that in the long run the way in which we treat others will be the way in which we are treated by them.

History is full of examples of men who have lusted for power, and used it ruthlessly and cruelly. For years they seem to get away with it, but in the end their fate usually is to fall through a more violent force.

Jesus, as usual, does not simply tell us that we mustn't judge others harshly and be over-critical; He gives us a hint as to how to avoid adopting such an attitude.

He says: "Be honest. Before you look critically at others, examine yourself. Look at your own faults, and search your own motives."

If we follow the advice of Jesus, such an honest self-examination will make us much more generous and kindly disposed towards others. Knowing our own weaknesses, we shall sympathise with others; being sorry for our own faults will make us sorry that others fail, and we shall want to help them out of their failures, and not condemn.

Such a gentleness and humility of spirit ought to be the distinctive badge of all of us who call ourselves disciples of Jesus Christ.

Suggested Bible reading: Matthew, chapter 7, verses 1 to 5.

WITHHOLDING THE GIFT

I HAVE a charming daughter of twenty-one, and it always gives me great pleasure to give her a present. I love to see her eyes sparkle when, after one of my visits abroad, I produce a necklace, or something of the sort. Being a person, she is able to appreciate the beauty of something that she is given.

But I do not go out to the pig-sty and give the pearl necklace to the pigs. They would prefer acorns.

Jesus, using the same metaphor—"Give not that which is holy unto the dogs, neither cast ye your pearls before swine" —warns us against offering that which is valuable and precious to those who will not appreciate it. To disregard this warning is to show a sentimentality and generosity which is not Christian.

We come across many instances of this in life. The doting mother who gives a small child an expensive and elaborate present; the child doesn't appreciate it in the least. He merely destroys it, and knocks it about. But give him a simple toy and he loves it and cherishes it.

An earnest Christian offers the riches and truth of Christ to some cynical person who has no sense of need whatever; with contempt he rejects any thought of Christ.

I am sure that many of us from time to time should speak and act to others gently but firmly, refusing to offer that which is valuable until they are willing to receive it. "It is no good my giving this to you or saying this to you just now; you just won't value it nor appreciate it."

Such an attitude will often bring the other person round to see how precious to the one who possesses it is the guarded truth.

In these days values and moral standards everywhere

around us are being lowered. Those of us who believe that something is utterly worth while and want to hold to it have a tremendous responsibility. We must never try to over-persuade other people to accept what we see as valuable; if we do, we only tend to lower its value in their eyes. Nor must we ever reduce the terms on which this valuable possession may be achieved or discovered. This action is to cheapen it.

What the world needs to see to-day are men and women who keep their values high and lofty, who hold them with dignity and cherish them as precious. If these values are really worth while, then others will gradually begin to respect them and desire them, to seek them, and in the end will be willing to pay the price to make them their own.

Suggested Bible reading: Matthew, chapter 7, verse 6.

KEY TO AVAILING PRAYER

JESUS is quite clear that prayer will be answered. He doesn't hedge round this subject with "if" and "perhaps" and "maybe."

Quite categorically He says, "Ask, and it shall be given you; seek, and ye shall find; knock, and it shall be opened unto you."

He is so sure about the love of our Heavenly Father that He knows He will not refuse to give an answer to one of His children who truly turns to Him.

It is this definite and incisive faith which is the key to real prayer. The Christian is meant to be confident, though humble, when he comes to God to seek His help and to offer his service.

But Jesus is careful to remind us that although we can

come confidently, knowing that God will answer, there is need for perseverance and determination: "Everyone that seeketh findeth, and to him that knocketh it shall be opened."

The thought here is that we may not find at the first attempt of seeking, nor will the door necessarily be opened at the first knock. If we really are determined to place ourselves and our needs in the hands of our Heavenly Father, then we shall go on with our praying until we are certain that He is dealing with the matter.

In the spiritual life I think we can truly say that we shall discover a certainty in prayer if we really want to discover it. I don't mean simply that if we want to get something when we pray, then we shall get it if we want it enough. There are things which God does not mean us to have, and therefore we shan't receive them; but there can be an inward assurance that He is answering our prayers, and dealing with us and the situation in His wisdom and in His love.

Suggested Bible reading: Matthew, chapter 7, verses 1 to 8.

A POSITIVE RULE

IT is sometimes said that one religion is as good as another, but I find that people who make such statements usually know very little about any of the religions, often not even one! There are great differences, and some are very much better than others.

Among the moral precepts of the religions we sometimes come across a principle which runs something like this: "Don't do to others what you don't want them to do to you." This is quite an admirable principle, because, for instance, if you don't want to be hit, don't hit other people first. It is good common sense.

In Christianity, however, Jesus turns the rule round, and makes it into the Golden Rule. "Do to others what you would like them to do to you." This is positive, and more far-reaching.

It is interesting to notice that Jesus bases this principle on the idea of a family. What kind of father, He asks, would he be who, if his son was hungry and asked for a slice of bread, gave him a stone instead? Or in place of a piece of fish handed him a poisonous snake? He would be no father at all, says Jesus, if he acted like this.

But fathers don't do that kind of thing; even though they are human, imperfect and sinful, yet they still treat their children properly and look after them.

In precisely the same way the Heavenly Father will look after His human family and His earthly children.

If this is so, then Jesus tells us tnat we who are members of the Father's family must do to each other the kind of things which we would like them to do to us. We must treat each other well and generously in exactly the same kind of way as our Heavenly Father treats us.

Suggested Bible reading: Matthew, chapter 7, verses 9 to 12.

THE NARROW GATE

We are not all going the same way home, and it is not true to say that it doesn't much matter how we behave, for everything will turn out all right in the end.

Jesus made it quite clear that every man has got to make a choice. He has got to decide for himself the direction that his life is going to take. If we will we can follow the way of the majority, going with the crowd, doing as they do and talking as they talk, seeking the things that we can touch and see, living only for the good things of life.

This is the broad highway along which many people go, and which, says Jesus, leads inevitably to the destruction of the soul of man and of his spiritual life.

There is another road, and it has a narrow entrance. It is the way of self-sacrifice and dedication. It is the pathway of self-surrender and dedication to God. It is not easy, for it demands an effort and a willingness to be different from other people.

Yet, says Jesus, it is a road which leads to the discovery of real life, to the finding of a true purpose for our existence here on earth, and to the knowledge of the spiritual world and of God Himself.

We must notice that the people who have started on the narrow way are by no means perfect: they still falter and they still stumble as they seek to lead the Christian life, but they are facing the right direction, and their feet are firmly planted on the right road.

Notice also that they are a minority—that Christianity will always be the religion of the minority. Dean Inge once said: "There will never be an inconvenient crowd at the narrow gate."

Suggested Bible reading: Matthew, chapter 7, verses 13 and 14.

THE TEST OF SINCERITY

DEEDS and not words are what count. To talk about God and to speak about Christianity by no means prove that a man is a real Christian. Sincerity is shown not by what we say, but by how we act.

This is a fundamental point in the teaching of Jesus, and He brings it home to us, as He often does, by the simplest of illustrations.

"If you have got a thorn bush at the end of your garden you certainly wouldn't expect to walk up to it and pick a bunch of grapes. Look at those thistles in your field. If you bend down over them you won't find figs growing there. If you want grapes, go to the grapevine; if you want figs, turn to a fig tree."

If we want to know of a man's sincerity, we must look at the fruits to be found in his life. If we notice some of the fruits of the Christian spirit, then we can believe that he is a true Christian.

Paul gives us a wonderful list which is true to the spirit of his Master. The fruits of the Spirit are "love, joy, peace, long-suffering, gentleness, goodness, faith, meekness, self-control."

No Christian is free from faults, however sincere he may be, but we should, if we know him well enough, be able to discern in a fellow Christian something of the spirit and mind of the Saviour; in his life we should be able to see some of the fruits of the Spirit, and to recognise that he is depending on the power of God.

Such a Christian, when he seeks to speak about his religion, may fail to be convincing by his words or by his arguments; but the witness of his life will be convincing.

Christians ought, of course, to try to be able to give a reason for the hope that is in them, but in the end it is the fruit of good living which is the greatest argument for the truth of the Christian faith.

Suggested Bible reading: Matthew, chapter 7, verses 15 to 30.

DEEDS—NOT WORDS

The other day I heard of a young couple who had been married for perhaps two or three months. The girl was a very genuine Christian; the man decent and straight, but he never went to church.

He knew she was a Christian when he married her, and so was not surprised when, after the wedding, on the very next Sunday, she asked him to go to church with her; but he refused. Each week she asked him; each week he refused.

He had no strong convictions against church-going; it was simply that he could not be bothered to do what his wife wanted him to do. Yet he said he loved her—in fact, he does profess to love her. Why then doesn't he do quite a little thing which she wants him to do, and which would please her?

I don't think much of profession which doesn't lead to action, do you?

Jesus Christ doesn't either. In fact, He says in the Sermon on the Mount that the man who professes to be a disciple but doesn't carry out his discipleship in his life is not only wicked, but foolish.

He is like a man who, building a new house, doesn't bother about foundations. Because it is cheap and easy he sites his home upon the sand, and, of course, in a moment of storm and flood the house collapses.

How much better, said our Lord, is the sensible man; he founds his house upon a rock, and nothing can shake a house so securely based.

There is a storm which most of us forget, but of which Jesus often reminded His hearers. It is the crisis of the Last Judgment. This greatest storm of all will not overwhelm a man of faith.

But faith is not a matter of saying, "Lord, Lord, I am Your disciple." Faith leads to action—the right sort of action, which is doing the will of the Father of Jesus as best we can, day by day.

Then, says Jesus, the man who has built upon the rock of moral action done to carry out God's will, will stand the test. The man who merely professed, will hear the tragic sentence, "I never knew you. Depart from Me."

Entry into the Kingdom of Heaven is by action, and not by words.

Suggested Bible reading: Matthew, chapter 7, verses 21 to 27.

III
THE TOPICALITY OF THE TEN COMMANDMENTS

A MORAL LANDMARK

Moses on the top of Mount Sinai is said to have received the Ten Commandments, engraved on two tablets of stone, from the hand of God Himself. With these in his hand he came down from the mountain and gave to the people of Israel the Law of God. It is a very strange story as you read it in the Old Testament.

Christians differ about this story. Some of them think that it happened exactly as the Bible tells it, while others believe that the story is an allegory. Moses climbed up the mountain to be alone with God; while thinking and praying he himself wrote down the Ten Commandments, which he believed were God's Law.

Whichever is true, the fact remains that the Ten Commandments became to the people of Israel the will of the Lord their God—and what magnificent commandments they are, when you remember the period of history in which they were given.

Stealing and killing often happened. Parents frequently were not respected, but neglected; and if you wanted something belonging to your neighbour, you got rid of him and took it.

In this kind of moral situation the Ten Commandments became a landmark. As the people of Israel shaped their lives in accordance with their teaching, they became a nation different from the other nations among whom they lived; not only did their worship of God become more spiritual and simple, but their community life was marked by honesty, neighbourliness and fair dealing.

This difference was part of their witness to the world that they were indeed God's own people.

It is sometimes argued that because we know the teaching of Jesus, the Ten Commandments have no value for us to-day. This, I believe, is wrong. Even a casual look round the world shows the need for us not only to know the Ten Commandments, but to *do* them.

Which is why I intend to take the commandments one by one to try to show what value they still have for us to-day.

Suggested Bible reading: James, chapter 1, verses 22 to 27.

THE WORD OF THE LORD

"I AM the Lord thy God."

This is the word of the Lord and the first of the Ten Commandments. And clearly, it must be the first commandment, for until we have settled that the Lord, the Living God, is going to be our God, there is no point in discussing His commandments.

If once we have settled that He is going to be God to us, then we shall know that we ought to obey Him. And presumably we shall want to.

This brings us up against a difficult problem, but one about which we must try to think and about which we must reach a definite conclusion. It is simply this. Why should we obey the commandments? Or, to put it more theologically, what is the basis of moral standards?

Some people will tell us that whatever helps us to live efficiently and well, that is right. It is good, for instance, to diet wisely, take sufficient exercise and to sleep well. These rules are binding because they make the body efficient.

For a similar reason we ought to be kind to people and not harbour resentment against them. Why? Because it is observable that if we harbour resentment against others we are not happy ourselves.

You can see where this argument leads. Moral standards are good and right if they make for efficient biological living, both of body and of mind.

Others would have us believe that the good is whatever furthers the objective of the group or the Party. This is the Communist view.

In both these theories, which are of the same nature, there is some truth. Goodness will always make for happy living, but if we believe in God we must see that that which is good is not right and good simply because it makes us happy and well, but because it is the Will of God.

Now you must not think that God just wills something to be right and therefore it is right. It is rather that because of God's own character, the nature of His own Being, certain qualities and attitudes are right through being in tune with the character of God.

If we believe this, then the commandments of God are binding on us because they come to us as the Will of God. If we obey them they will help us in a small way to build our characters after the likeness of God's character and assist us gradually to become sons and daughters who reflect the likeness of their Heavenly Father.

Suggested Bible reading: Deuteronomy, chapter 6, verses 3 to 14.

BE RIGHT WITH GOD

"Thou shalt have no other gods before me." God must be first, for if He is Lord at all, He must be Lord of all.

This is not simply a religious sentence; it is plain common sense. If we believe in God with our minds, we must treat Him as God in our lives, and honestly seek to allow Him to control us.

It is a great pity, I think, that people, especially clergymen, often try, as it were, to bribe us to be religious. Perhaps they put it like this: "If you want to be happy, then put your trust in God, for He can take away the burdens and sadnesses of life, making the pathway easy."

Quite frankly, stated thus it is not true. Of course, if there is a God, then it follows that only when we trust in God and are right with Him can we live properly as men and women should. We become really ourselves, for if He is our Creator, then we, His creatures, can only realise our true natures and live our true lives when we are rightly related to Him.

This will make us, I am perfectly prepared to agree, truly happy in a deep sense; but, on the other hand, in some ways it may well turn out that our lives do not seem to be as happy as they might appear to be if we were living care-free, flippant, pleasure-seeking lives, regardless of God or man.

After all, it doesn't always make a child happy to obey his father's wishes, but if the father is a wise father, in the long run it is far better for the child to behave like that than to be disobedient. It is exactly the same when we are dealing with our Heavenly Father.

The first commandment tells us that we must live in obedience to God, the second points out that there cannot be "other gods" in our lives; we must not have idols or graven images.

I can almost hear some of you saying, "Don't be silly. Imagine my putting up a little idol on my mantelpiece."

Of course you wouldn't do that, but it is very easy to have mental idols—ideas or things that we really worship instead of God. What about the god of money, or of the T.V. set? What about the idol of self that we see in the mirror every day? Sometimes you will find people who worship other people more than God—for instance, their husband or their children. And what about the large-scale idols—those we call ideologies—which put the State above God or man?

Oh yes, it is very easy to let many things get in front of God, so that we may say with our lips that we believe in God, but in our lives we are really putting our trust in something other than God, and giving our true loyalty and love to that.

Suggested Bible reading: Exodus, chapter 20, verses 1 to 17.

TAKING GOD'S NAME IN VAIN

IN America, High School boys and girls always ask me questions. "Is it wrong to swear?" is one of the favourites. My usual reply is, "It depends what word you use."

I must be honest and say that I don't mind an odd "damn" or two, though I think it gets very boring if someone can never talk without using it as an adjective, whether the subject is good or bad.

Filthy language, of course, is always wrong, and it is a great pity if children aren't trained to be careful about the way they talk.

Yet even this isn't, I believe, quite so bad as to break the

BEING AND BELIEVING

second commandment and to take God's name in vain. Two ways there are in which we can do this.

Phrases like "O Christ," "O God," do in fact break this commandment, yet how frequently we hear people in ordinary conversation, as well as on the stage and in films, casually use the name of the Creator and our Heavenly Father as a mere exclamation. Somehow we should be revolted, I think, and rightly so, if we found ourselves using merely as an exclamation the name of some human being we loved very much.

One summer on the beach in Italy two Christian ladies were sitting near an Italian who was constantly saying, "O Christ," or "O God," and so on. At last one of the ladies got up, went across to him and politely asked him his name. It was "Bruno."

For the rest of the morning she kept on saying to her companion, "O Bruno," "Good Bruno!" in the normal course of her conversation. After a while the man could stand it no longer. He came across and said, "I wish you would stop using my name! I don't like it. It irritates me."

"Well," she replied, "I wish you would stop using the name of Christ and God, because I don't like that either." The upshot was a friendly conversation, and the man saw the point. He was a good fellow, and was only just being thoughtless.

Are you being thoughtless and breaking the second commandment without meaning to?

Suggested Bible reading: James, chapter 3, verses 1 to 9.

TALKING TO GOD

We break the third commandment by using God's name as an expression of our feelings—in surprise, in exasperation and in anger. There is, however, another way by which we can also break this law of God. Many professing Christians often fall into this trap, a thing easy to do without realising it.

Jesus warned us of it when He told us not to pray using "vain repetitions" as the heathen does. When we talk to God in prayer we mustn't be careless and "just say words." We must think about the Person to whom we are speaking— it is God Almighty we are addressing—our Heavenly Father, and yet the Supreme Creator. We must therefore take pains about what we say, we must mean the words we use.

It is at this point that we can so easily take God's name in vain. We can, for instance, drop on our knees and say, "O God, bless me and all whom I love," etc., etc. Carelessly and casually we say words we have said many times before, without a single thought about the Person to whom we are talking. This is to take God's name in vain.

Or we can ask God for things which are quite preposterous because they are completely contrary to His character. I have known people in bitter hatred and resentment actually ask God to harm another person.

If, perhaps, they have not exactly asked that harm should happen to them, they have prayed fervently and long that they might get the advantage over the other person. Such a prayer is an attempt to twist God to one's own ends. This is the taking of His name in vain.

When we pray to God or sing His praises it is our business as reasonable human beings to take the trouble to think about

Him, to consider who He is and what His character is. Then we shall be reverent in our attitude to Him—not otherwise.

Suggested Bible reading: Matthew, chapter 6, verses 5 to 8.

DO YOU GIVE SUNDAY TO GOD?

THE fourth commandment—"Remember the Sabbath day, to keep it holy"—is one of the most difficult for us to understand and to keep. Amongst religious people there has been, and still is, a great deal of controversy, as to its true meaning.

If you read it carefully you will see that part of the commandment is obviously localised—that is to say, refers to the particular situation in which the Jewish nation found themselves when Moses presented them with the Law of God.

The words refer to a farming community which gave hospitality to a passing stranger who happened to be within their gates. Theirs was a patriarchial order, with the married sons and daughters and all their families living grouped together with all their possessions round the grandparents.

In such a self-contained community it was quite possible to do no work at all on the Sabbath day, except, of course, for the satisfactions of elementary needs. Such a day of rest was obviously of great value.

It always is useful to leave behind the chores of everyday life and to be able to relax for a period. Moreover, such community rest enabled all the members of that community to take part together in the worship of God.

It was a real witness to the whole nation and, perhaps even more important, to the neighbouring nations living alongside, that God was their Father and that they were trying to live as His children.

But the situation to-day is much more complicated—notice I don't say better, I merely say more complicated. We have our electricity, gas, transport and other benefits of civilisation. All this work, it appears, must go on without a break.

Moreover, many people work throughout the week, and the Sabbath is perhaps the only free day. If they want to enjoy themselves, see their friends and take part in sports, then, necessarily, extra work is caused to others.

This is the complicated situation which we face when we try to take seriously the fourth commandment. We must first examine the question of Sabbath versus Sunday, and then we are ready to try to find out in what way we can best keep this commandment.

Suggested Bible reading: Exodus, chapter 20, verses 8 to 11.

GOD COMES FIRST

SOME people are worried as to whether the weekly day of worship and rest should be observed on a Saturday or a Sunday. The Jews naturally observe the Saturday as their Sabbath, and some Christians think they ought to do the same.

The fourth commandment laid down for the people of Israel that one day in seven should be set apart for rest for the body, for recreation of the mind, and, above all, for the worship of God. This was the seventh day.

The people of Israel carefully observed their Sabbath, finding that such obedience gave them spiritual strength, and was a witness to the surrounding nations.

The first Christians were Jews. In the early days of their

Christian experience they kept the Sabbath, but they also met together the following day, the first of the week, for their own fellowship meal, the Holy Communion.

They chose the first day in remembrance of the resurrection from the dead of Jesus Christ, their Master.

As they began to realise that Christ alone was the foundation of their faith, and that no longer need they observe Jewish customs, they dropped the observance of the Sabbath, but continued to keep the first day of the week for worship.

Moreover, as Gentiles who had not been brought up with Sabbatical customs became Christians in increasing numbers, they brought pressure to bear upon the early Church in the same direction.

To them the important point was the keeping of one day in seven for the worship of God; which day of the week they counted as the seventh really didn't matter.

For us Christians Sunday is the Sabbath. It is our privilege and duty to keep it as a day of rest from work as far as we can; as a day of recreation for our minds, and, above all, as a day for the worship of God in company with our fellow Christians.

One of the tragic developments of this century is that here in Britain we are losing the sense that on Sunday the worship of God comes first. This is our biggest failure in the keeping of the Sabbath.

Suggested Bible reading: St. Mark, chapter 2, verses 23 to 28.

YOU AND YOUR CHILDREN

BROKEN homes and divorces seem to be news for the popular Press. Happy marriages and successful families never are.

One would almost think that we had very few contented

people living in the homes of England, but, of course, we have.

Our prosperity as a country has been firmly built on stable home life, wise parents and contented children. And this is not only true of our own country. It has always been true, ever since man lived upon this earth—the family has been the unit round which human life has revolved.

It is this principle that is so firmly underlined by the fifth commandment. "Honour thy father and thy mother that thy days may be long in the land which the Lord thy God giveth thee." What could be plainer? The prosperity of the nation is bound up with the honouring of parents.

After all, a successful family, where children are taught to do their duty and to show respect to father and mother, is laying the foundations for those same children, when grown up, to carry out their adult responsibilities and to respect their fellow citizens.

Wise, loving parenthood will produce co-operation from the children. That same attitude of wisdom and love in national life will sweeten and guide relationships between employers and employed.

It is clear that the principles of religion are the principles which really work in daily life if only we will apply them. Religion is not something imposed from above by an arbitrary God—it is the natural way of living.

And, of course, it must be so. If God there be at all He must ordain the natural way of things—the natural order, as the theologians call it.

Family life—training for citizenship. To-day, perhaps, some of our citizens are not as good as they might be. The remedy lies with the parents and in the training given in the home.

Suggested Bible reading: Ephesians, chapter 6, verses 1 to 10.

HONOUR THY PARENTS

"Must I do whatever my parents tell me?" An interesting question posed by a seventeen-year-old girl with unsympathetic parents. What is the answer?

"Honour thy father and thy mother," says the Old Testament. "Fathers provoke not thy children to wrath," says the New Testament. Somewhere between these two statements lies the truth.

It is all a matter of attitude. The right attitude of children should be one of happy, loyal obedience to their parents, respect and reverence being given in response to love.

The wise father and mother will always treat their children from the very beginning as reasonable persons. Of course, it is quicker and less troublesome, to say, "Do this because I say so," but it is far better, when one can, to explain the reason why such and such a thing is right, or why such and such a thing is wrong. Time and trouble spent in doing this are never wasted.

Such wise treatment will gain a ready response from the average child. Better still, as the child grows older he will tend to become reasonable because he has been treated reasonably. By this means the wise parent keeps the confidence of the growing child.

Such a relationship will rarely produce a head-on clash. Later on, however, a situation is likely to arise where the parents' wisdom—or perhaps sometimes prejudices—will dictate one course of action while the adolescent will desire another.

I believe we parents have to be prepared for the youngster to go ahead and learn by his own mistakes. We shall only "provoke to wrath" if we are heavy-handed.

After all, provided we don't say, "I told you so" if a mistake is made and we parents are seen to be right, it will strengthen the bond between us and the erring child. Common-sense though this may sound, it needs to be said because it is often forgotten.

It must be added that young people too easily fall into conceit, and imagine they know everything. Such disrespect for experience is stupid as well as wrong.

The commandment "Honour thy parents" is one God means us to keep—and keep it we should.

Suggested Bible reading: 1 John, chapter 2, verses 10 to 14.

CRIME OR PUNISHMENT?

THE sixth commandment, "Thou shalt do no murder," raises the problem of capital punishment. Recently the condemnation of an eighteen-year-old man to death raised a furious public controversy. He committed murder in a fit of passionate abandon. Guilty of the act he clearly was; but should he have been hanged?

Let us put on one side the peculiar circumstances of that particular instance, and ask ourselves the simple question, "Does the inflicting of capital punishment conflict with the sixth commandment?"

This is a perplexing moral question upon which Christians have found it very difficult to make up their minds. It is sometimes suggested that we have capital punishment because society is trying to revenge itself upon the killer. This, I think, is rather a far-fetched psychological explanation.

I am sure most of us who are reasonable citizens would

only wish to defend capital punishment if it deters potential murderers from committing the crime.

We want to prevent innocent people being killed. That is why we support capital punishment, certainly not from any desire for revenge. But strictly interpreted, I think we must allow that judicial killing does weaken the sixth commandment.

It is possible to argue—and many good Christians do, and I am inclined to do so myself—that in certain circumstances judicial killing may be the lesser of two evils. If it will prevent the greater evil of more wicked men killing innocent people it may be justified.

We therefore are faced with the question which seems to me the only one that matters—does the death penalty prevent murder by acting as a deterrent?

I am becoming increasingly doubtful as to whether it does. Those countries where capital punishment has been abolished do not seem to have found that murders increase. Of course, social conditions may be different, but it is a significant fact.

Once it can be established that capital punishment does not deter, then it ceases to be the lesser of two evils, and is a sin which should be ended finally and immediately.

Suggested Bible reading: Matthew, chapter 5, verses 17 to 24.

THE MAKING OF THE CROSS

THE supreme instance of the breaking of the sixth commandment—"Thou shalt do no murder"—was the crucifixion of Jesus Christ. This, if ever there was one, was a case of unjustifiable murder.

For three years or more Jesus Christ had lived a life of service and love. He had moved amongst the people freely and simply, healing the sick, and teaching God's way of life. He had not claimed any special privilege for Himself, had little money, and often nowhere to sleep.

His one aim had been to be perfectly obedient to the will of His Heavenly Father, with the result that His life was one of sheer goodness.

His teaching set forth the highest ideals for human living the world has ever known. He pointed out that motive often coloured morality more than the act. For instance He showed that hatred of a brother man lies at the heart of murder—and therefore that the hating thought is in itself the breaking of the sixth commandment.

The very challenge of the life of Jesus stirred up hatred in the hearts of the self-complacent Pharisees, and anger in the minds of the common crowd, who merely wanted Jesus to satisfy their selfish material interests. So Jesus became unpopular, and in the end was put on the Cross and killed.

Yet the death of Jesus is not simply the unjustifiable murder of an innocent, good man. It is, as Dorothy Sayers has said, "The execution of God by man in time and history." For the life of Jesus was the life of God lived out here on earth.

Yet the horrible truth is that when ordinary men and women like ourselves came face to face with the life of God they hated it, got angry with it, and finally made an end of it —or tried to.

If we are honest, searching our hearts, we all know that we are no better than the actual crucifiers of Jesus; we are sinful people like them who hate God and try to put Him out of our lives and make an end of Him.

We have all had a hand in the making of the Cross.

Suggested Bible reading: Isaiah, chapter 53, verses 4 to 9.

THINK RIGHT

"Thou shalt not commit adultery"—and some people think that if they haven't they are pretty well free from sin. But there are two points in Our Lord's teaching which these people often forget to face.

First of all, although Jesus completely reaffirmed the seventh commandment and made it quite clear that adultery was wrong, yet the main emphasis of His teaching was to suggest that the sins of the spirit were equally bad, if not worse than the sins of the flesh.

Think how He slated the Pharisees for their arrogance and pride. Think how He turned on those mean, bitter people who, instead of rejoicing at seeing a man healed on the Sabbath Day, were so narrow that they thought only about the breaking of some convention connected with the Sabbath.

As someone has said, Jesus dealt more severely with the sins of respectable people than He did with the frailties of the human flesh.

The second point which is often forgotten is that Jesus gave a much deeper meaning to adultery. Though to Him the adulterous act was certainly wrong, He also regarded the lustful desire, if allowed to remain in the mind, as wrong. "Whosoever looketh on a woman to lust after her has committed adultery with her already in his heart."

This aspect of Our Lord's teaching is of the utmost importance—it is part of the original quality of the Christian religion. In His eyes the motive is as important as the act, the thought as the deed. "As a man thinketh so is he."

This is why the sincere Christian who truly seeks to follow the teaching of Jesus and live by His Spirit is always conscious of failure and inadequacy. His standard is so high and challenging. We may be able to avoid committing the act; but how few of us can escape from thinking the thought?

The key to success here is not to steel our will against the act and leave it at that, but by prayer, worship and Christian action to allow the Holy Spirit to guide and direct our thoughts, so that we are able to think right, to share in some small measure the mind of Christ.

Suggested Bible reading: Philippians, chapter 4, verses 8 to 13.

HONESTY IS THE BEST POLICY

IT used to be said that the English people were the "honestest nation on earth." In all parts of the world an Englishman's word was taken as his bond. Our word could be trusted, and our integrity was taken for granted.

I'm afraid it isn't quite the same to-day. Everywhere there is a decline in standards of honesty and truthfulness.

Recently I lunched with one of Her Majesty's Judges, and he remarked that in his opinion the multitude of regulations and restrictions had encouraged the majority of the nation to become "pilferers." I'm afraid he is right.

I believe it is still true in England that major dishonesty and corruption don't exist on a large scale amongst us. Public men and civil servants by and large are scrupulously straight. Most of our business men play the game with each other, and keep up high standards of integrity. And ordinary folk like ourselves don't yield to the temptation of shop-lifting. We generally tell the truth, and are quite reasonably honest.

Yet for all of us there is a moral danger in the small

BEING AND BELIEVING

"pilferings," in the exaggerations and prevarications, the white lies and the petty dishonesties practised so often to get round petty bureaucratic regulations and restrictions. In the end they do undermine our high standards of honesty.

Perhaps they don't affect older people quite so much, but I am quite sure that young children and young people who are brought up in this post-war moral atmosphere must be affected by it; and this is a very genuine and serious danger.

God's commandment, "Thou shalt not steal," is an absolute one. Honesty and respect for other people's property are binding upon us, and we certainly must not try to water them down.

One of the best contributions that we can make right now is to be sure that our own standards are kept high, and that we refuse to pander to minor dishonesties. To train our children in straightforwardness and scrupulous honesty is thoroughly worth while.

In the long run honesty *is* the best policy. It not only pays, but it is right; and there is great satisfaction in choosing the right, and carrying it through.

Suggested Bible reading: Romans, chapter 13, verses 7 to 10.

DON'T THROW MUD

Few of us would willingly commit perjury. We would recoil with horror from the very thought of standing up in a law court and swearing away a neighbour's character.

Such deliberate condemnation of another, falsely and unjustly, is repugnant to all decent people.

But the ninth commandment, "Thou shalt not bear false witness against thy neighbour" covers far more than such deliberate acts of betrayal. There is idle gossip, the spreading of a careless rumour. What about this? Doesn't it also fall under the condemnation of the commandment?

There is no doubt that it does, and rightly so, because such gossip causes far more harm and hurt than deliberate perjury. Why? Because it is far more widespread and common, and also because it is almost impossible to catch up with it and lay it low.

You know the old phrase, "Throw mud and some will stick"; it is perfectly true—a wild story about somebody, a rumour or piece of gossip which defames his character, and something will remain, even when the statement is shown to be false.

One of the most impressive ways in which Christians can show that they are different from other people by reason of their religion, is in their total abstinence from gossip and the spreading of unfounded rumours about their neighbours. I am far from sure that such total abstinence is not more important than total abstinence from alcoholic drink. The intoxication of gossip is more heady and harmful than wine; and its evil consequences may be wider spread.

St. James, you will remember, in his Epistle says that the tongue is a small evil, but like a spark, it can start a prairie fire. In villages, in streets, in a factory, in a Women's Institute, even, alas, in a church hall, such malicious and careless gossip can ruin a community spirit, can create suspicion in a home, and can destroy real friendships. Nothing perhaps can make people so unhappy as being talked about unjustly.

Here, then, is a point in life where Christians can bear a real witness, and can help others to do the same. Such action is not simply a keeping of the ninth commandment. It is going beyond it, and offering a service which is acceptable to Christ.

Suggested Bible reading: James, chapter 3, verses 1 to 10.

SEEK GOD FIRST

"I WISH I had a frock like hers." "They've got T.V. next door; I wish we had a set like that."

In speaking like this, are we breaking the tenth commandment, "Thou shalt not covet . . ."? I don't think so.

When the commandment was first given, the danger of coveting any of your neighbour's possessions—his lands, his cattle, his wife—was that in a simple society covetous thought might well lead to aggressive action—to seizing the land by force, to strife, to fighting, and even to murder.

If the community were to be a happy and peaceful one it was therefore tremendously important that men should learn not to envy their neighbours' prosperity, nor covet their neighbour's possessions.

To-day, in a more law-abiding society, envy hardly ever leads to violence. Most of us have got clear of gangsterism in our behaviour.

We can't conclude from this that the commandment is out of date, however. It still has something to say to us. Envy and greed are subtle sins. If we are possessed with the idea of trying to keep up with our neighbours and their material prosperity, if we must have all the things they have, and fashion our lives on their style, then imperceptibly we become people who judge life by material standards, and begin to think that all that really matters are the things that we possess.

Such an attitude makes for real unhappiness. It produces strain and worry, and an urge always to be making more money that we may get more and better things. Such envy can bring bitterness into a home, and resentment, for instance, into a wife's mind towards her husband because he is not doing as well as his next-door neighbour.

Besides, if we can't get what we want by fair means, we are tempted to try the foul and so to get set on the pathway of dishonest business or shady tricks.

No wonder, then, that our Lord condemned covetousness in no unmeasured terms, and warned his disciples to cultivate a mind which sought first the kingdom of God, and was content with the material goods that came naturally and straightforwardly.

In this materialistic age, the commandment "Thou shalt not covet" is needed as much as ever, and the Spirit of Christ, which can set us free from such envious thinking, is available for all who desire to keep this commandment.

Suggested Bible reading: St. Luke, chapter 12, verses 15 to 21.